ROMANIAN NOTEBOOK

# Romanian Notebook

CYRUS CONSOLE

FARRAR, STRAUS AND GIROUX
NEW YORK

Farrar, Straus and Giroux

120 Broadway, New York 10271

First edition, 2017

Library of Congress Cataloging-in-Publication Data

Names: Console-Șoican, Cyrus, author.

Title: Romanian notebook / Cyrus Console.

Description: First edition. | New York : Farrar, Straus and Giroux, 2017.

Identifi ers: LCCN 2016025811 | ISBN 9780865478305 (paperback) |
    ISBN 9780374713195 (e-book)

Subjects: LCSH: Console-Șoican, Cyrus. | Console-Șoican, Cyrus—
    Family. | Authors, American—21st century—Biography. |
    Console-Șoican, Cyrus—Travels—Romania. | BISAC: BIOGRAPHY
    & AUTOBIOGRAPHY / Personal Memoirs. | BIOGRAPHY &
    AUTOBIOGRAPHY / Literary.

Classification: LCC PS3603.O5577 Z46 2017 | DDC 818/.603 [B]—dc23

LC record available at https://lccn.loc.gov/2016025811

Designed by Abby Kagan

Our books may be purchased in bulk for promotional, educational,
or business use. Please contact your local bookseller or the Macmillan
Corporate and Premium Sales Department at 1-800-221-7945, extension 5442,
or by e-mail at MacmillanSpecialMarkets@macmillan.com.

www.fsgbooks.com • www.fsgoriginals.com
www.twitter.com/fsgbooks • www.facebook.com/fsgbooks

*for Paula*

ROMANIAN NOTEBOOK

T*inus*, a Latin suffix forming adjectives from adverbs of time, for example *pristinus*, "former," "previous," "ancient," "old," from classical Latin *prior*, "in front," "previous," "former," "earlier," "elder," "superior," "more important."

Often I start a work of writing by looking up key terms in the *Oxford English Dictionary*, a practice whose chief virtue is that it leaves the work itself unchanged.

Thus *pristine*, "unspoilt by human interference," "untouched," "pure." "Of something natural," the entry stipulates. Or Old French *crastin*, "the day after (any feast)," from *crastinus*, "morrow," from *cras*, "tomorrow."

For "tomorrow" is an adverb of time.

•

We leave in turmoil because Paula's nineteen-week ultrasound has shown a bright spot in the fetal heart, "in baby's heart," as the technician phrases it.

Fifteen minutes pass in no particular order; the young doctor arrives. Everything looks great, she says, I am required to say, to talk to you about this one thing, the bright spot here, in baby's heart, which is associated with increased risk for Down syndrome. Your numbers are still overwhelmingly good.

I say, can you tell us more quantitatively about what this does to our risk. The doctor crosses her arms over her chest. I want to high-five you for these numbers, she says.

I try to keep her in the room while I come up with a concrete question to put to her—a process my mounting alarm makes both urgent and impossible, and as a result of which, I think, whatever memories these moments form are recorded either in such a manner, or in such a location, as to render them mostly inaccessible now, in the days or years that follow.

I say, tell me what term, in order to learn more about the bright spot, we would need to put into the search engine.

"Echogenic intracardiac focus," thought to result from calcareous mineral deposits in the tissue, transient and effectively meaningless. I get out something about "plans for the pregnancy should further blood work indicate chromosomal abnormality." The high style into which I find myself slipping is a strange, dependable symptom of my anxiety.

I think about Du Fu, China's greatest poet, so they say, how he fails the civil service exam owing to the intricacy of his prose, then waits eleven years before making a second attempt, in 746, the year the prime minister, probably to discourage rivals, grades every exam as fail.

"And the second half of that sentence is," the doctor says, a turn of phrase I experience as hostile. Maybe I have interrupted her—maybe the literary speech has offended her—I forget what comes after this. At or beyond gestational age of twenty-two weeks it is forbidden, she says, in Missouri or Kansas to terminate pregnancy.

In my days as father-to-be I feel among midwestern medical professionals, with their unvarying diction of "this white band here is baby's little diaphragm, and these are baby's little toes," that when I speak the word "fetus"—a term descending through a cloud of much older terms related to nursing, sucking, and bearing fruit—they judge me already as baby killer, or worse, atheist, and now that I ask about abortion explicitly I bear the weight of this judgment, illusory or not, the more heavily.

But I must think of it as a fetus, never as a baby, because there remain so many weeks in which miscarriage or worse, progressively worse, feels likely to occur, and to lose a fetus would be a very different thing than to bury a child. I read nurses' discussion forums about fetal demise, stillbirth, how long to allow the mother to stay with the body, hours, days, how to advise her of natural processes of degradation and decay.

•

The phrase clings and turns like a bright wrapper in a stream, "mental retardation." I am aware it's no longer viable. The end came during the American vice presidential candidacy of Sarah Palin, minor political figure for whom the so-called special needs family served as talking point.

Nowhere does semantic degeneration take on clearer outlines than in the discourse of intellectual disability, intellectual developmental disability, and no discourse is more salutary to the posture of the primary-school student fighting for social dominance, so it is on the schoolground and in the context of neurodevelopmental disorder that I learn this process, also called pejoration, by which, however honorable their intentions, words become offensive.

"Moron," "imbecile," "idiot." "Retard." "Cretin," for example, cognate with "Christian," "which in the modern Romanic languages," the dictionary says, "means 'human creature' as distinguished from the brutes."

We are in the waiting room of the lab, 1296- or 1728-point script on the wall in the color sometimes called seafoam reads *Extending the healing ministry of Christ*. In twenty-four hours we get on a plane; Paula hits twenty-two and then twenty-three weeks while we are in Romania; I'm about to describe not what I believe is necessarily right or appropriate but, again, what I think or feel, the terms in which I think and feel it, namely that for reasons I have not begun to fathom, for us to bring into the world a mentally retarded child is unacceptable, categorically. And yet, despite my understanding that the risk is small, it seems to me the process has already begun.

Outside, where I can get my phone to work, I stand beside a metal chair and try to contact our obstetrician, Lomax, who the nurse says will call me back later today. I start consulting my phone every ninety seconds or so, though I have no idea what I want to say to Dr. Lomax. I dial Ben, the first letters of Ben's name, which makes me feel guilty about having left Paula behind in the waiting room. So I call my mom, who is at our house watching Sylvie, our one-year-old, the baby.

Paula has left the waiting room by the time I get there. I find her at the valet parking stand. Home, I behave so anxiously that she tells me to go on a bike ride, a position she has never taken before, since—compared with my former avocation, running—cycling is a time-consuming and dangerous way to stay in shape. But now that my knee is apparently wearing out, it's the best I can do. A man with a retarded son would have no time to himself, I think.

I speak to Ben just before the bike ride and develop with his counsel a clear set of objectives for the phone call: I need only establish with Lomax a plan to abort the pregnancy if blood work indicates, and amniocentesis, presumably, confirms, Down syndrome. Or worse. I put the phone in a handlebar bag and crane my neck until my ear is right up against the zipper, trying to make sure I am not missing the call from Lomax while I ride.

The cars seem to pass faster and closer than normal. I ride about sixteen miles, pedaling out to the Indian Creek Trail and back on my blue fixed gear, but no call comes.

When I get home, in the durable light, I mow the lawn with our Finnish reel mower, and then, since my legs are so tired, break my rule about driving to school, where I arrive about 9:00 p.m., when on any other night I would be in bed. But, as with mowing the lawn, I feel I have no choice about watering the plants in my office—not with three weeks' vacation looming—except the terrarium, which looks all right. So I drench the hoya, the crassulas and euphorbias, various succulents I have been meaning to identify.

I make to leave, but as I lock the door behind me I hear the winding sound of the AC turning on—the old three-story house containing the Liberal Arts offices has been fitted with an institutional AC unit, with the result that every room is maintained at a temperature either excessively hot or excessively cold, almost incredibly hot or cold. In the summer my office is sometimes 45 degrees Fahrenheit. I keep a sweater hanging on a thumbtack beside one of the sway-backed bookshelves. However, the worry now troubling me is not about extremes of temperature to which my plants might be subjected, but rather the extreme dryness of the conditioned climate, the dehydrating effect of the industrial volumes of cold dry air periodically flooding the office. Calculating with intense effort, I let myself back in.

I pride myself on a certain endowment of technical ingenuity and dexterity, and at times, especially in moments of anxiety, discover energy or drive to put this to use. I stand on a chair; in my hands I have the bin liner from the office wastebasket. I unscrew the single machine screw affixing the register to the wall, place the plastic bag over the duct, and replace the register so that the liner forms a seal. I turn the screw back into place and, exchanging the can opener/ mini screwdriver for the small spear point blade on the thirty-year-old Victorinox Spartan I keep in my desk, a knife my father gave me for my seventh birthday, I trim the protruding parts of the liner from around the metal frame of the register, taking something like pleasure in the thought that my knife must be scratching the paint on the wall of this building in which everything is pointless, and which houses the L-shaped office conferring onto me the inglorious status of expert among undergraduates.

Just to say to myself the phrase "my knife" fortifies and reassures me somehow, as if of my place in an uninterrupted lineage of capable men.

I think of the school painter, a slight man with a narrow, tight plait descending the nape of his neck. This painter, I'm told, a man with whom I have not exchanged a word—though I have often engaged him in polite negotiation of the space in which we prosecute our mutually incompatible professions—has been diagnosed with stomach cancer, weeks to live.

Favoring my left knee, I get down from the chair. In a version of my own voice swollen with the kind of bluster I suspect marks my classroom manner, I hear the phrase "gastric carcinoma."

Probably because of the extreme agitation that typifies my teaching style I have no clear image or memory of myself actually teaching, but I hear myself pronounce the words "gastric carcinoma" as if I were lecturing on *The Death of Ivan Ilych*, a novella I've assigned many times, though I haven't really given a lecture on it and am not even sure what a lecture is, strictly speaking, let alone a novella.

By the time I drive home it is 9:45 p.m. I have neither packed nor made other preparations for the trip. Dr. Lomax has not called. I reason with myself in my dispiriting way, feeding out a customary line about efficiency, about handling the task more effectively in the morning, and therefore, by postponing the work, better husbanding my time. Why spend ninety cranky, muddleheaded minutes packing now, losing valuable sleep, when I might accomplish as much in just thirty next morning with a clear head and cheerful countenance.

More than cheerful, since I will be rushing on four cups of coffee, brilliant thirty-year plans springing forth effortless and fully formed amid the billions of surplus cycles of my throbbing brain. But even as I lay out this rationale for the delay I know its real motivation is a desire to protect my mood—not that it is a good mood, quite the contrary. Yet the worse my mood gets, a decline typically starting mid-afternoon, the more pressing seems my need to maintain it, to keep it from further harm. I climb into bed.

•

Most of my correspondence games are on a three-day clock, three days per turn. Despite Paula's request that I turn off my phone and sleep, I feel it would be, for lack of a better word, irresponsible not to make a move now, to move in each of my twelve correspondence games, even the seven-day games against players like Dr. StrangeGlove and Zwischenzugs who for whatever reason prefer this more dilatory schedule.

I should move because who knows what delays might arise during the two travel days ahead of us. Otherwise

I will be cutting it too close. Plus, the sense of urgency induces a presence of mind that makes the task a pleasant one, and with my mood so low and vulnerable as it is, I owe it to myself to take pleasure or comfort where I can. Who knows what could happen while we are aloft.

I put my knee up on one, then two pillows and assay, thinking explicitly in these terms, to determine whether the knee is "pain free," but find myself unable to tell if what I feel is pain, or merely discomfort. And if mere discomfort, then how can I tell if it was there when I lay down, or if the pressure of scrutiny is itself making the joint uneasy.

It's coming back to me now, or I go back to it, or out to meet it in the farther shadow containing everything that happens, how I tell my primary care physician, a fit man by the name of Huff, that I don't believe there are any issues really except for the knee but figure I should retain a primary physician, that is, establish an official relationship with one, that Lomax recommends him, and I respect Lomax. I'm concerned about my knee, I say, slipping partially into the high style, because I rely on cardiovascular exercise to—and running being the only form that really works for me—moderate the anxiety and regulate the mood.

I get it, Huff says, a phrase he turns out to use whenever he needs to describe someone who also understands or relies upon physical exercise in this way. I can send you to a good orthopedic surgeon; we play racquetball; he gets it. Just as he opens his mouth I interrupt: actually, I have to give readings several times a year, for example this year a couple in New York and one at University of Chicago, you see, I'm a professor of English, that isn't even strictly true, why do I say that, why am I saying any of this if not from some sense of inferiority, in my youth it was assumed I'd become a physician. More than once in conversations with strangers I have claimed to hold a PhD in English, it just slips out, as if I can't bring myself to say "in creative writing."

I experience a lot of anxiety during the readings, I say, and beforehand, but worse is being on the plane, on the plane I experience what could legitimately be called panic, so if you could prescribe me something for these types of occasions. Huff smiles patiently. I can see that he is, without a second thought, going to write the prescription, and though my heart does not stop pounding, the quality of the pounding changes from that of a criminal about to be apprehended to that of one about to escape.

I strike a tacit bargain with myself to take the pills only for readings and air travel. As husband and father I feel I can look back without passion on the spectacle of the three-day blackouts into which, in the checkered past, I converted similar prescriptions. You can put those on, Huff says, indicating my trousers.

•

In Kansas City International, a circular complex of terminals whose occupants are afflicted only in that, without hope, they must live on in a state of desire, I shake a few milligrams of alprazolam into my palm, then, in Detroit, some more, then some in Amsterdam, and some, apparently, in the lavatories of the last plane or planes, and consequently cannot exactly account for how we arrive at Henri Coandă International, drive five hours to Paula's sister's apartment in Roman—the apartment she, Gabriela, shares with her husband, Bogdan—and, after some hours of putting Sylvie to bed, sink into a dreamless slumber. I know from experience, experience generally speaking, that I will have enjoyed the flight, savoring while it lasts a mellow regard of the silence reigning in that tract of my mind normally occluded by panic dread.

Thursday, at any rate, I wake about 09:00, convinced something has happened to Sylvie, convinced it is Wednesday, though, in the face of whatever catastrophe, strangely composed. Sylvie is sleeping peacefully.

The next time I go in to look at her she is standing at the bars of the crib. I spend the day minding her while Paula and Gabriela run errands like getting waxed or changing money. At 16:00 we drive to the village of Rotunda to see Cristian and Elvira, the grandparents.

It is not the gradual shrinkage and rustification of commercial infrastructure that indicates we have entered
the village, but how the children and adolescents in the
street never seem to be going from one place to another,
only looking up from their conversations, conducted
normally in threes, to watch us pass in Bogdan's little late-
model Opel.

The house stands in a giant garden of grapes, straw-
berries, raspberries, apples, potatoes, onions, beans, and
other produce, chickens. I notice the new porch and breeze-
way of pine studs and cedar particleboard, built not as
contractors build but as a homeowner does, with greater
care and lesser sureness of hand. My parents-in-law come
out to meet us in the courtyard and, waiting my turn, I
greet Cristian with a prepared phrase congratulating him,
Paula later informs me, on attaining the status of primate. He receives this graciously, probably understanding
I mean to refer to his being elected, some months ago, to
a prominent post in the local government. With a kind,
worldly air he offers me his hand.

I recall our first meeting. It takes place in this garden;
I am looking into the sky over my father-in-law's left
shoulder; we are embracing as part of a formal greeting. I
have just planted my lips on his neck, not, as I had antici-
pated, on his cheek, since the embrace brings our heads
too far into each other's space for that; I am staring into
the sky over Cristian's shoulder, the grape arbor over the

yard next door, his brother's yard, because I have just realized that Cristian is in no way prepared or disposed to reciprocate such a kiss, contrary to my assumptions, since this ritual greeting requires no kiss and maybe does not condone one.

After stowing our bags I have a hard time making myself turn and walk back down the stairs, or rather, I turn several times to face the stairs without then taking a step in their direction. From my window I see the church, the gardens of three houses, the roofs of more, as well as the large white building adjacent to the church, the priest's house, I guess. The rooftops vary on themes of tile or sheet metal. I think about the house belonging purportedly to the Bulibașa, which we pass on the outskirts of Roman, and which boasts an astonishing roof of sheet metal imbricated like the scales of what I think of as the national fish—the carp—and bulbous Slavic turrets or cupolas, everywhere fringed, trimmed, and crested with scrolled and filigreed sheet metal resembling galvanized lace. I suppose that such elaborate roofs, which I see clustered on the perimeter of villages like this one, are traditional among Romani families.

I lose ten minutes looking at the garden walls. One is red corrugated steel, apparently repurposed from a shipping container. One, orange stucco, crowned with three strands of barbed wire; another, cloudy plexiglass framed by a simple rectilinear arrangement of welded steel rods, whereas the fourth, just barely visible, accomplishes with the same rod-and-plexiglass construction elaborate ornamental triangles and circles. The walls range between two and three meters tall. If I walk down the block, as I do, later, under a full moon, while the village sleeps, I see further walls made of decoratively cut boards, or of sheet metal and rods, plexiglass, and so forth.

Between these walls and the road stretches a narrow margin of grass, shaded by the occasional walnut or willow and three varieties of cherry: the small sour cherry; the dark bitter cherry, from which is made a delicious preserve tasting almost like chocolate; and what I think of as the default cherry. Some authority has installed benches where, during the late afternoon, older people sit with no apparent object. Every hundred meters or so from this margin there rises a cylindrical well, often painted in bright colors, outfitted with a roof, a windlass, bucket and chain, sometimes also equipped with a cast aluminum drinking cup that shines dully on its lanyard.

Children, of which the street is now full, pause their ball game periodically to drink here, first filling and offering the cup. I listen to the bustle downstairs without detecting any sound that seems to refer to my absence. I need to get the wireless password from Cristian. I'm thirty-five years old, I think to myself.

•

Thirty-six, I think. Subvocally I repeat the word "compensation," hesitating again between the window and the top of the stairs, compensation, which, given a true sacrifice not part of any immediate tactical combination, is the big question, so far as I understand it, in chess.

White lacks material, but has more than adequate compensation in the form of mobility or positional advantage. "Chess figures placed in a passive position have no plastic or aesthetic appeal." I see a dim image of subtitles beneath the face of Marcel Duchamp. "It's the possible movements that can be played from that position that make it more or less beautiful."

Now, I ruminate, is when not having spent years practicing something begins to cost dear, now is when it really begins to be possible to have spent years and years failing to practice. In this moment and in moments like it I feel my chief ambition is to live long enough either to forgive myself for not having made use of my potential, or really to see and make peace with the fact that the potential is, and was, unexceptional.

Chess is a game fundamentally involving time: not the time of the clock, but the spatialized time of the board itself. Whether or not the king can complete the standard endgame task of running down a pawn, for example, is typically calculated by picturing the fleeing piece at the corner of a mental box, the so-called rule of the square, the perimeter separating "in time" from "out of time."

Time and space in chess are liquid generally, but in the person of the king they achieve perfect equivalence. This above all other reasons seems to me to account for the king's centrality. The queen, for example, is the most powerful major piece because for a given unit of time, the turn or move, it has the broadest choice of destination, the most freedom with respect to space. A pawn, on the other hand, is structurally incapable of occupying more than seven squares in any game. No matter how hard it works, this pawn will never see most parts of the board, not even given infinite time.

For the king, however, every unit of time is also one unit of space, and vice versa. The king spends much of the game waiting. Games sometimes end before it has moved.

Of course the clock is also important. Blunders, for example, in grandmaster-level chess occur most typically on the thirty-eighth or thirty-ninth move, since in many tournaments crucial minutes are added to the time control only once the player has reached move forty. This problem has various names: time trouble, *zeitnot*.

Surely I have not spent them, surely it is impossible that I have spent these years in true idleness, not I, who have so much on my mind, I think. No one has given more thought to the question of how to begin.

But how can I hope to accomplish any of the major achievements, books, mostly, which I have vaguely planned for myself, before I truly understand and accept the fact now confronting me, namely that for the first time I am less agile, less strong, less sharp than formerly, and that it is in this direction things continue.

They asked Altenberg's father was he proud. "When he did nothing for thirty years, I never let it get to me. So now that he's a poet, I can't say I'm that impressed. My gift to him was freedom."

My hope is that certain kinds of experience, "long experience," will enable me, will give me unanticipated— but "powers" is not yet the word, since my only example of progress so far, an example more affecting to me probably than it should be, the fact that I can now, in the dark, that simply by holding the shirt in front of me, holding it at the shoulder seams, unseen, I can discern, by means not entirely clear to me, which way the shirt faces, and thus put it on properly—"powers" is not yet the word.

I can entertain the hope of compensation, hope for the influx, by deep remedial force, of subtle means to solve problems whose dim presences have so far obstructed my goals, whatever the goals have been precisely. Though I am for the first time in my life's journey palpably stiffer and slower with the passing day, a mortal taste in my throat, like stagnant water, or the smell of stagnant water rising sometimes into my nose, yet I no longer put my undershirt on backward.

•

In other ways I still move about the world as a child. In Rotunda, for example, I drink bleach—bleach procured from Elvira for the purpose of cleaning Sylvie's sippy cup, the flexible silicone straw of which is clogged with black mold. Siphoning it through the straw, what am I thinking about, something far off, I take the bleach into my mouth and, not before I realize what is happening, but before I can react, swallow.

I am not harmed by the experience, only impressed that it or one like it has taken so long to befall me. I can report that bleach is slippery in the mouth. High pH solutions are known to be slippery. It is also salty. But the fact of sodium hypochlorite having this characteristic should never have shocked a man of my education.

Doamna Elvira, I say, using the form of address that makes me feel like a schoolboy, but which I understand to be the most appropriate of those available. Doamna Elvira, I say again, turning a corner into one of the new additions or partitions of the household. Again she makes no answer, though I can now hear her behind a frosted glass screen, washing something with a splashing sound.

Doamna Elvira, I say very loudly, I have reserved the bleach in a, in a, but, unable to think of any word for "container," I trail off. With an abruptness unfamiliar to me, she responds what I assume is the equivalent of "Okay," something she would do probably in any circumstance but especially if she has understood no part of what I said, the usual outcome of my speeches to her.

With a faint sense of irritation I take yet another step into the room and say again, even more loudly and slowly, so much so that my voice assumes surreal proportions, Doamna Elvira, I have reserved the bleach, I have reserved the bleach, lapsing hopefully into silence. This time she makes no reply. I can see her holding very still behind the frosted glass. Only after I turn to leave the room, as I am coming out into the part of the patio where the table and chairs are, where we usually eat, do I realize she is seated on the commode.

•

I have long hoped or intended to write a book about the manchild, a historically significant type into which I believe I can offer real insight. Unfortunately the only materials I have thought to include are scattered memories of Kirby and Dale, manchildren of my childhood, Kirby not even a manchild strictly speaking, only the local itinerant schizophrenic. I don't know why he figures in all my child-hood memories. He was never in one place.

Certainly the book would have to include an account of the year I spent in the house on Connecticut Street, the year, as I increasingly think of it, of the disorder, the condition developing during my most thorough and sustained effort to conquer procrastination, a regimen of self-improvement in which for three years I prepare unsuccessfully to win admission to a PhD program in "theory and criticism," swallow amphetamines every few hours, and come to rest playing Internet Scrabble in boxer shorts, shirtless, shirt on backward, all night alone in a house with a vaporizer cooking on the mouse pad and a Sig Sauer P228 in my lap. My opponent goes on to write a notable book of anagrams derived from Shakespeare's sonnets.

Paula is calling me. I head downstairs. We eat dinner and go to bed and the next morning return to the city of Roman. A retarded son would have no potential whatsoever.

•

In the city I guess it's a point of hospitality that the television in an occupied room be left on, volume low enough that the content is audible without being intelligible. At dinner Gabriela switches to TVR Cultural, a channel broadcasting what appears to be a talent show or recital. The emcee, a broad rectangular woman with a sober permanent and a starched white shirt tucked into a dark woolen skirt, does her job without affectation, upstaged by the giant shadow of herself visible on the white wall that composes more than half the shot.

Paula, Gabriela, and Bogdan talk animatedly about some unrelated thing. I feel myself growing extremely tired and, as is frequent with me, irritable, irritated that I am tired, practically enraged at the fact of being tired, yet forbidden, by my probably miscalibrated instinct of politeness, from excusing myself.

I feel it would be offensive in the extreme for someone in the position of the silent husband to eat the delicious food, shift his weight a few times in the armchair ordained as his place at the kitchen table, and from which the corner of the nook it's placed in partially obscures Bogdan, to the right, from view—so that as he sits back, cutting Bogdan entirely out of the picture, he must somehow give further offense—then, speaking for the first and only time, make it known that he wishes to retire and leave them to their unfathomable conversation.

I ease myself deeper into the armchair and, giving up on trying to comb vocabulary from their talk, allow myself, as inconspicuously as possible, to follow the proceedings of the talent show, its two shots alternating between the woman with her enormous shadow and the floor by the microphone stand, place of tribulation.

In his handling of the keys the pianist, age fourteen or fifteen, seems driven by a priority of avoiding any sign of weakness or effeminacy. He is succeeded by one, and then another, violinist, the first playing each note both under pitch and slightly too far from its neighbor, so that it sounds like she is on a sled moving rapidly away from the observer, as in a physics experiment.

The second violinist plays with great seriousness, having chosen one of the two or three most cliché recital pieces for violin, probably the utmost cliché in the context of a violin recital, a composition supposed to move dramatically between frolicsome passages and ones of mournful beauty. Maybe the name of the piece or its composer will come to me. I think the title refers to the fact of its melody being appropriated from folksong. I think it has the word "Gypsy" in it, problematic word.

Her playing transports me from the rapid, superficial tempo of daily life into the profound and virtually still time frame of stage fright, where in the mind of the afflicted performer one thought overwhelms all others, so much so that the particulars of the score seem tiny and remote as drowning persons, strangers for whom one would unhesitatingly risk one's life, in principle, but whom one could not possibly reach in time—a lifetime would not be long enough to reach the scene of their accident. The thought is that the dreaded time is now.

The suspicion that this moment has revealed in you, the bystander, great and noble potential—this knowledge, coupled with the fact that no speed could wing you to a place where you might enact the heroism latent in yourself—produces a depersonalized sensation like that following the public receipt of a great compliment, a longed-for but unhoped-for recognition. Since adolescence I have mentally reenacted such scenarios, never concretely defining the terms of the compliment, but rehearsing its acceptance with great solemnity.

I fear that if and when my obscure merit is finally celebrated, I will endure it as if I were fourteen years old, namely by freezing in my tracks with a grave, almost scornful expression on my downcast face, a tactic which in my youth I believed capable of suppressing all show of the pleasure welling up in me. I can see now of course that the tactic's real effect is simply to broadcast violent suppression of pleasure and pride that, but for the concomitant wish to conceal it, would be innocent, faultless. And this response has become automatic, over years of conditioning taking place almost entirely in the long and circular train of my thought and not through any traffic in actual compliments, and my grave facial expression or the feeling of embarrassment and shame to which it correlates has supplanted any available pleasure.

•

Later there is a "cloud rupture" and from my place on the sofa in the guest room I watch purple light suffuse the thunderheads and, what seems a moment later, reveal the facades of the neighboring buildings. The apartment blocks of cities like Roman have in their decidedly state-constructed appearance an aspect common to project housing throughout the hemisphere. To me they express the childhood feeling associated with a certain kind of present, a gift that is not the wished-for gift, but rather what a parent could afford, and therefore radiating always the bittersweet aura of the parent's hectic praise.

I lie on the sofa, increasingly intruded upon by thoughts about the special relationship that must exist between Romanian household dogs and their short, ever-present tethers. By 05:30 I feel very tired, having had to keep vigil with the baby the night before from 00:00 to 03:00 and then simply lain awake until dawn. Then there is another night in which the baby will not sleep. I spend much of it on my back, on the floor of her room, touching her hand through the bars of the crib, or rather allowing her to touch mine, something she accomplishes with much pinching and gouging, using her tiny sharp nails. It occurs to me that I have long since lost track of the passage of days.

Part of tonight's trouble stems from my drinking, at about 19:30, a long double shot of espresso, which I justify, not in the best faith, as remedy against my extreme somnolence, an espresso made possible because just as Paula and I are taking the baby on a walk another cloudburst overtakes us and we shelter in Cofetăria Tosca, owned by our acquaintances Gelu and Dora, a large, smart pastry and coffee shop in whose enclosed terrace, mostly empty, two groups of people sit smoking and drinking beer. Each group includes one or two pregnant women, though I don't see whether these partake in the smoking or drinking. I open the large windows all the way, until the rain falls in on us, but can't evade the billows of cigarette smoke.

Even as I put the cup to my lips I have the seasoned drug user's experience of an exceptionally good, maybe lethally good batch of product, and over the next hour I fly into an intense, intent euphoria, even speaking in my fashion to the people behind the *cofetărie* counter, something I would not normally attempt. At the moment, though, I have the need, or not the need so much as the opportunity, to pee, and in my tweaking condition that provokes brisk action.

I also review mentally the positions of all my correspondence games. For a moment it seems to me I can recall each position with total accuracy. First-rate players do this as a matter of course and can even play blindfolded, something that was at first incredible to me.

My own mental image of the board involves only key tensions or combinations and omits many pieces and structures, though with practice this image grows slowly clearer and more comprehensive. I wonder if the best players experience the blindfold schema of the board the way I do, as primarily kinesthetic, that is to say not as visual images, but as vectors of movement and force, typically shifting or evolving in a definite rhythm, doot, doot, doot, doot, doot.

My hobbies or hobbyistic obsessions, pastimes whose power against time or time management is colossal and shattering, all share this quality: that they function as retreats into a place of visuospatial fascination, realm over which language has no dominion. For example, lying on my back, waiting for sleep, shrinking my awareness almost to a point, like the smoking focus of a convex lens, I linger, sequentially, in my mind, over every articulation of the mechanism of a late 1980s bicycle that I own or, more typically, intend to own. Earlier in life I knew comparable intimacy with the mechanisms of firearms or folding knives; I look back on that now as a status from which I have progressed. But the arrival of this propositional train of thought in itself signals that my focus has crept irremediably out of the maze of the chessboard or the derailleur and into the verbal wasteland of rumination.

Certain bearing assemblies—for example in old bicycles—being shielded from contamination by what is referred to as a labyrinth seal, my focus turns now, and turns again, to the figure of the labyrinth. It is a wall, fundamentally, it serves as a barrier, but topologically the labyrinth contains nothing, there is no place where the wall closes itself, no separation of interior from exterior. The interior is a temporal distinction. The wall is functional without being actual. What detains or imprisons the wanderer is mere delay. The maze is a barrier that is also an occupation, and is one only by virtue of being the other—not a walled-off place, but walled-off time. That is what I think of, suddenly, as my "idea" about the labyrinth. I try to remember something about Theseus but instead visualize Jack Torrance with the fire ax, here's Johnny.

I think of the coffee in Stifter's *Rock Crystal*, an almost magically strong decoction intended not for the young sister and brother, who are only relaying it to the next village as a gift for their parents, but which saves their lives all the same by postponing fatal sleep, riveting them nightlong to the fierce beauty of the ice field in which they have lost their way.

Back at the apartment, reclining on the floor by the baby's crib, I worry more pointedly about the fetus. The grim thoughts that intrude on my most anxious spells now intrude: when I close my eyes, the darkness fills with sense images of my own body jerking at the end of a rope or more likely some improvised halter, like a dog leash or extension cord; or it fills with the image and sensation of vaulting over the guardrail of a bridge, the instantaneous attendant regret of this, total regret; or the sensation of the muzzle of a gun placed first here, against the raphe between nose and upper lip, an anatomical feature called the philtrum, and now here, in the soft hollow under my jawbone, in efforts to align the path of the bullet with my brain stem. I feel the chamfered bore of the short-barreled .357 revolver I no longer own grow warm from prolonged contact with these ports of call.

Some traditions hold that the philtrum is a mark left by the angel who strikes your face just before you are born, obliterating all memory of your life as a soul.

I remember the conversation with Ben in Pittsburgh where we are walking around the reservoir, a pileated woodpecker crosses the sky, I can't see it really, the bird is just a dark spot overhead describing the species' signature undulant flight, I am experiencing what I can describe only as a series of verbal accidents in which my tone, despite myself, grows despondent and then I say to Ben, I bought some, some, faltering. Go on.

Well. Well, let's see. A Glock 19, the SP101, the GP100, a little Kel-Tec 9mm, a Remington 870, the P228, another Sig, a P6 decommissioned from some force or agency in Europe.

No, of course not, I respond to the one question Ben, after a pause that seems to cost him, puts to me.

But as I say this I realize that not only have I thought about, think about it routinely, but that I bear in mind, for example, a definite ranking of these guns in terms of their suitedness for this most statistically representative of purposes.

•

Our second Saturday morning in country I go with Bogdan to the *piaţa*, asking him about words to describe the weather as we quit the stairwell. Bogdan is a very perceptive person. Well when it is like this, seventeen, eighteen degrees, but he stops there, hefting the bag we are to drop off at the dumpster. Silently I note the three two-liter plastic bottles placed on top of the kitchen waste.

We-e-ell, Bogdan says, in his characteristic way drawing out the discourse particle, we don't manage to sort our trash here—he means of course not "manage" but "bother." Why not, I ask. Well, he says, we have so many people searching in the trash, meaning scavengers, scrappers. And what difference, I say, pushing my luck, does that make?

Well, he explains, if we sorted it they would only mix it up again.

I try to picture a destitute person transferring materials across the platform from the recyclables dumpster to the trash dumpster or vice versa in a way that could possibly repay the time and effort this would require, and the thoughts pass into a consideration of how, in Bogdan's willingness to cite as justification against his contributing toward some public good the supposed misbehavior of a category of disenfranchised people, I perceive a fundamental of the conservative type.

I notice he is wearing his office clothes, slacks, patent leather belt, ironed white short-sleeved button-down with a dark tie—to me his ties seem aggressively narrow and short—his phone, cards, cash, and some volume of other essentials in a brown leather clutch with polished metal fob, and I can't help feeling, though I dismiss the embarrassing idea from my mind as soon as it arises—it arises repeatedly—that he has subconsciously forgone his usual weekend attire just to let me feel the difference in our positions, the greater degree to which he has assumed personal responsibility, responsibility in the abstract.

He stops the car in front of what must be a bank or ATM; I don't turn my head. I will return very quickly, he says, poking his head back in just before closing the door. Take your time, I urge him. Well, he says, I thought we had a hurry. The manner of macho bonhomie I now assume disgusts me even as I assume it. Paula, I say, might have a hurry, but for me this, meaning the errand, is a vacation. Bogdan gives a polite laugh.

When we pull up to the bustling open-air market I ask, thinking again of his outfit, and of the word, *răcoare*, for

the mercifully cool weather, and feeling a rush of grati-
fication at the thought that a full week has elapsed, the
trip now seems almost manageable, well, Bogdan, what
are your plans on such a nice Saturday. He gives me a
more definite version of the quizzical look I feel has somehow underlain our whole morning's conversation. What
will you do today, I rephrase the question, now that it
is Saturday.

But Cy, he says, it is not Saturday. It is, he pauses almost
imperceptibly, Thursday.

We pass into the marketplace, which I experience distantly,
involved as I am in a private struggle with this setback.
What I notice of the market is row after row of identically
stocked stalls, each brimming with two kinds of large
sweet or bell pepper, carrots, potatoes, tomatoes, eggplant,
and onions. I check the ceiling—we are moving deeper and
deeper into a sort of arcade—to reassure myself that no
specialized lighting has been installed there. The vegetables look so vibrant that it produces, for me, an optical illusion of the presence of what I assume are the very expensive
lamps used by the more exclusive American grocers to
render the colors of their tomatoes and carrots according
to neuro-economically optimal bands of the spectrum.

All above me, and because it is Thursday I don't look
closely, nor am I receptive to what I see, but there hangs
a translucent ripstop fabric, typical tarp fabric, or maybe

a fiberglass composite sheeting, arching over each aisle. It is a little bit impressive to me how we continue to move deeper into this space, especially given the ambiguity of our hurry or lack thereof, and I wonder how a city as small as Roman can support so many vendors of so many indifferent vegetables. When we finally reach the other side of the space and emerge into the overcast street, I am surprised to find us standing at Bogdan's car, precisely where it was before.

He gives me a ride back to the apartment and I carry the groceries up the stairs and put them on the table in the entryway, regretting that the two liters of milk, kilo of carrots, kilo of peppers, two kilos of tomatoes, and kilo of eggplant, plus five hot peppers to eat with soup, have cost me not more than ten dollars, as I fail to see how I could ever offset, at this advantageous rate of exchange, the burden of our presence in the apartment. But I am very happy to see Paula, and I tell her, shaking my head and laughing, about Bogdan and the Thursday thing. Paula laughs energetically in response, in the fondly scornful tone that Bogdan, even mention of Bogdan, seems to provoke in her.

But it's not Thursday, she says. Today is Friday.

•

I am supplied very little information about what keeps Paula busy here but my intuition is that it has something to do with missing paperwork. We have allowed her passport to expire, for one thing, and we also need to get a birth certificate, a Romanian birth certificate for Sylvie, something we've been meaning to do for thirteen months now, months during each of which, courtesy of the state, we could have been accruing one hundred euros in an account established in Sylvie's name. But I know that Paula leaves each morning, usually late in the morning, with her father, who, each day, arrives after what seems to me to be a long and theoretically unnecessary logistical negotiation carried out between them over the course of several phone calls.

Saturday we drive to Rotunda to smoke meat. On the way into the village we pass long views of meadows interspersed with linear stands of poplar, beech, linden, or locust. Overnight there has been another cloud rupture, flooding Buruienești, and the trees have an immodest, storm-tossed aspect, swathes of foliage showing the silvery undersides of leaves.

We pass several of the horse-drawn carts standard among a poorer class of laborer here, and I am reminded of the striking experience of passing such carts on the road in winter, the winter air, in which the archaic sound of hoofbeats and harness bells is subjected, by the differential speeds of cart and car, to a pronounced Doppler shift, a sound effect quintessentially modern even when it accompanies the whistling of CGI arrows or cannonballs in blockbuster features set in the Dark Ages. But for whatever reason, differences of impedance I guess, the sounds travel differently, travel seemingly not at all in the warm and humid atmosphere of June.

As a rule I feel so low at the moment of waking, probably in large part because of withdrawal from caffeine, that I tuck into the caffeine with abandon. This morning, having jolted myself awake—no other way ever seems possible—with first one, then a second cup of strong coffee Paula brought me, soon enough I find myself overwhelmed with more of the same extremely unpleasant anxiety about the fetus, or about Sylvie, a living being, who, it occurs to me, seemingly for the first time, must suffer and die.

But first, the initial hour or so of euphoria I am compelled to spend playing chess on my phone, in this case rapid chess, fifteen-minute time control. Or first I write this, fiddling with tenses while I deposit a heinous shit in Bogdan and Gabriela's bathroom, an enclosure whose air, at least when I am in it, seems instantly to saturate one's clothes, towel, and person with feculent moisture. I bang my head again on the cabinet and promptly resume my seat, cursing and rocking, face in my hands. Only then do I play chess, dealing an opponent by the name of Super-Santa a cataclysmic defeat after they castle queenside, moving the rook through my f5 bishop's diagonal, something which, amazingly, I had not realized was legal, and which causes me to run nine minutes from my clock in wonder.

Once I have satisfied myself through a polite chat window exchange that the rook, unlike the king and contrary to my previous understanding, can castle freely through lines of attack by other pieces, I mount an assault on SuperSanta's king, whom the disarrayed queenside pawns leave poorly protected, and in the course of six or seven moves, made with no loss of tempo, I exchange minor pieces, discover an inescapable threat on the queen, and force SuperSanta through a series of checks to trade rooks and maneuver the king onto even more perilous ground. SuperSanta resigns, we exchange pleasantries, my heart pounds through my shirt. I wash my hands and poke my head into the kitchen. Then, on pretext of putting the baby to bed for her nap, I lie on her floor and play chess.

I think of Vassily Ivanchuk, among the most brilliant players in history, a grandmaster famous above all for running out of time, for flagging, so termed because of the little flag on the old analog chess clocks: the minute hand pushes it higher and higher on its bushing until, the two parts reaching the limits of their radii, the flag falls, swings on its pivot a few times, and then hangs vertically, as if in a dead calm.

I go to the bathroom again, gastrocolic reflex, I think, and when I rise from the low, tilted seat of the toilet I bang my head again on the sharp corner of the cabinet. Later that morning as we pass through Buruienești I can't stop thinking about how if the fetus is mentally retarded, we will have to spend literally all of our money on airfare to return early for a traumatically and in most states illegally late-stage abortion. At thirteen weeks the fetus is the size of a mouse. At nineteen weeks it has grown by one order of magnitude, though it is still one order of magnitude smaller than a newborn. God knows what the experience will do to Paula. But at least we have Sylvie.

Twenty weeks, I think. Twenty-two. The night before an important game with Karpov, Ivanchuk stays up trying to derive a mathematical method for determining whether a number is divisible by seven. To hear him describe it, near dawn, the upwelling of "a such pleasant feeling" interrupts the seventh hour of his vigil. He "suddenly understands everything." In the event, Ivanchuk, playing as black, obtains a superior position but gets into severe time trouble. He finishes with a draw.

Now we pass an abandoned horse cart and I see the empty bridle wet-molded to the lineaments of its long-suffering animal, and now we pass a chow mix on a chain so short the dog cannot even rear back on its hind legs, not for lack of trying, and I conjure all of the suffering at once, both what I view as the organic, somehow minor, artisanal suffering of the current landscape, the quaint, rustic suffering that lends piquancy to my tourism, and the major suffering I associate with my home and compatriots, whose great innovation in torment has been to lend it deniability, delegate it, outsource it, factory farm and foreign war, death dealt indiscriminately by drone and captive bolt.

Reaching middle age—the one accomplishment in which I feel I am precocious—brings with it one change, the thing beginning some years back, when it seemed too much work to persist as a vegetarian now I was marrying a Romanian, and which I sometimes suspect—without allowing myself fully to investigate the suspicion—is slated to be my life's great moral failing, namely to say, yes, so much suffering, an ocean of suffering to which I contribute, whose tide I no longer make any effort to stem, grief, pain, and dread that overwhelm any love in the world and to which with each meal I myself add fresh blood, though I might choose otherwise. Less clear whether I can choose not to board the A330 strewing contrails of sublimated blood, the blood of obliterated Afghan wedding parties and Iraqi scavenger-children, but I will no longer make any effort to impede this suffering.

There is a passage in Cage's *Indeterminacy* where after a concert whose program notes include a statement about there being too much suffering in the world, Cage remarks to the composer that in his opinion there is neither too much nor too little suffering in the world, but "just the right amount."

I have a vision of myself as Baldessari standing in front of a boxy seventies-era camera and moving my arm minimally, first one way, then the other, turning slightly to face the camera with each gesture, and with each announcing "I am causing pain," "I am causing pain."

I guess the new thing is that the suffering does not have to be also mine. I look away, figuratively and literally, from the dog and his chain or the civilian with a blasted daughter in his arms, I can acknowledge this pain without choosing to feel it empathically, not feel any part of it after the very first shock of its recognition, which is not even really palpable, more like drawing back from a hot stove, a subcognitive neurological process that never ascends higher than the spinal cord.

The worst feature of this lapse is the calculus that I, too, will have a share in the suffering, not in the distribution of it, as in the present case, but in the receipt of it, that my portion of suffering is to come, that in the long view I will be one of the victims too, no meaningful distinction between me and the other animals marked for slaughter, no slaughter on my behalf. This also is a form of procrastination.

What draws my thoughts again and again down into the topic of suffering is not compassion so much as fearful conviction that suffering is pure, unalloyed participation. The rumination leads back to Leo, whose name we have lighted on without careful thought. Leo, the first name we discussed, the name that started a discussion on the subject

41

of names, a subject we then let drop, a name that as weeks passed attached itself securely to the fetus.

It seems to me that while the abortion of this twenty-two-week-old Leo, whose movements I now observe through the warm and pliant wall of my wife's body, would be awful, indisputably, even more awful would be to give birth to, and subsequently to raise, a mentally retarded Leo. That would be the worst-case scenario, I feel, and not least because we are destined not to be very wealthy, my salary is forty-five thousand and Paula might not be getting a job anytime soon, at this rate might not even finish her PhD. Horribly, a logic of destination resolves around the echogenic focus. The procrastination and lack of organizational capability that have plagued my adulthood now threaten consequences of a magnitude I have never before been bold enough to fear or even to suspect.

The salary is an outcome of this weakness. To put it frankly, without making claims for the accuracy of my judgment, I feel that a person with a literary mind as fine as my own should be able to achieve fame, I mean such as the literary world can bestow, and commensurate fortune, by his thirties. But instead I have spent thousands of whole days not writing word one of the notable, not to say great, works I privately consider as proven reserves. I have this teaching job, for which I am grateful, and some hundreds of copies of two slim, hesitant, and stilted volumes of poetry, or maybe not even poetry, but a kind of belletristic hand-waving that invokes poetry generically and achieves actual poetic effect only by accident, at least that's how it seems to me in the car on the way to Rotunda. I experience the whole project as a failure, a manifestation of severe congenital deficiencies in time management, self-discipline. Up until Paula's second ultrasound I am more or less fine with this. It is enough if I improve myself by practice.

I have always had the ability, when career or status anxieties beset me, literally to take a deep breath, look into the sky, whatever kind of sky there is, the sky never repeats itself, and feel in a deep and genuine way that not my name or rank, but the sky is what matters. And so when I am seventeen years old and I procrastinate my college application essays, so that what I submit are not essays at all, but frantic, bluntly penciled efforts to carpet the page between midnight and dawn of the day they are due, my mother, and this is the only time to my knowledge she has willingly induced another person to lie, asks the postal clerk to change the date, now that we have missed the deadline, of the postmark. And after she explains, with the feeling only a mother could inflect, our situation, the clerk does, I think, change the postmark.

So fare my applications to Harvard, Yale, Brown, and my dad's alma mater, Cornell, I who have long ago given up extracurricular activities in favor of whatever it is I do with my free time, or perhaps free time itself is my end of the bargain, instead of spending time studying or learning a skill I spend time experiencing it as "free," I seek the experience of free time, of freedom in time, with the single-minded determination of genius. But the ever-accumulating pile of contingencies gathering in the wake of this progress through life, or, more accurately, gathering like a shock wave at the nose of the projectile that I am, now results in a scheduling error that can ruin lives.

The uncanny swiftness of years, the ghostly silence said to characterize the experience of pilots in the fastest spy plane, positioned as they are in front of their own report, the beautiful name of a rapid eye movement, "saccade," the so-called stopped-clock illusion, chronostasis, familiar from earliest school days, which I remember mostly in terms of awaiting dismissal, the thousands of incidents of my seeing the red second hand twitch, so it seems, backward at the moment of my consulting the austere slave clock that graces the front wall of every classroom like a seal.

Ivanchuk is world champion in blitz and a dominant player in rapid chess until the federation announces that they will include blitz and rapid results in ratings calculations. At this point his blitz and rapid performance decline markedly.

A reporter asks him how long does it take for a normal person to make it to grandmaster. Normal people, Ivanchuk says, do not make it to grandmaster.

•

As we arrange ourselves on the patio where the meat-smoking party is to be held, Paula informs me that a father and daughter have been invited: he is an engineering professor in Iași; his daughter, whom Paula once tutored in French, has just finished medical school. In April, a subject expected to be sensitive, her mother, the engineering professor's wife, died.

The medical student, whose name I don't catch, arrives in green skateboarding shoes, baggy black jeans, and a black blouse that seems too formal for the ensemble. Once more, I listen intently for her name, so intently, as is often the case with me, that as I watch her lips form the word, my private exhortations to focus drown it out.

Her wardrobe has been dictated probably as much by obesity as by choice. In her arms she has an ill-mannered black poodle dressed in a too-small sailor suit and sporting two tightly knotted bows in the long curls above its ears. The student and her father come through the gate into the garden kissing everyone but me on both cheeks, left then right. I try to think what signal I have given, I am sure I have done so, that I am not to be kissed.

I can't tell if it is a trick of the light, but the student seems to have a coarse, closely shaven beard, particularly on the large doubling of her chin. I have the feeling which sometimes comes over me when I sit as an uncomprehending observer, namely that because I can't run the interference of small talk, and because my observation is correspondingly intensified or sharpened, the catalog of these observations, a running commentary, is plainly visible on my face.

I feel I can't so much as make eye contact with the medical student without communicating that I am meanwhile taking an inventory, peripherally but critically, of her features. Yet to avoid eye contact is worse, since it means that I have decided, with grotesque arrogance, that it would be kinder to spare her, spare her what, the shame of knowing herself observed by a being like myself? Or the awkwardness of knowing that one's visage, for whatever complex of reasons, potentially produces awkwardness in some viewer?

Obviously this is a mise en abyme, and it is too late now to undo it, to avert the cascade of slights and insults it will inflict throughout our interview. When I look, as if for relief, to her father, or at him, I perceive that his left earlobe is somewhat malformed, as that of a plastic figurine placed near a flame.

What rescues me temporarily is in fact the most interesting thing that happens to me in Romania: the sudden, novel conviction that I now experience my situation *as prose*, that perhaps because of all the writing I have done here in the passing days, behaving for what seems the first time in my life like a real writer, except that I am not writing anything special, just noting what comes to mind, or perhaps only because the situation prompts in me such pointed and explicit observations that they seem to exist as fully formed, somehow written, not spoken, sentences. Written, because I can move forward and backward in and among them at will, uninhibited by the ephemerality of speech, undaunted by the arrow of time.

The notebook, furthermore, especially because it gives the appearance that I am working, has become a failsafe against other forms of participation. Breathlessly I tell myself that I must cultivate this prose experience from now on and never let it go. This very advice I behold in stately, slightly ironic typeface.

•

I start wondering again about the beard, what it means that a medical student, someone who has in fact graduated from medical school, would not know or, more to the point, would not choose to pursue some expedient such as electrolysis or "laser hair removal," if that phrase refers to a viable technology, "laser" is such a scammy term. Would it represent a failure of national or personal wealth or resources? Or a national or personal triumph of values, a free and confident refusal of the all-corrupting vanity pervading my home culture? But by what right do I project heteronormative values on a stranger who might want the beard, choose it, and be happy with it.

I remember billboards popping up throughout Topeka to advertise "laser pain treatment" clinics, huge portraits of a lab-coated clinician smiling as if to say I know, and you know, what this is really about, but the squares perceive it dimly, only as an unnameable falling-off.

Finally I grow so uncomfortable that, with no means and perhaps no need of excuse, I rise and stalk behind the house to look at the meat smoker, doing my best to conduct myself as though my presence there is required.

•

The smoker stands in the part of the garden where the chickens are penned, thickset white ones for meat, red ones of less certain destiny, this year balefully afflicted with an avian mange. It consists of a sheet-metal chimney just taller than me, square in section, with four lengths of rebar spanning the mouth. From these, on sharp, soot-blackened gaffs, hang mackerel, racks of short ribs, hunks of pork belly. The chimney conveys smoke from a pit fire of beech and, as a latter resort, oak, over which more sheet metal has been loosely tented. I stand for a long time on the cinder block placed for that purpose beside the smoker, peering into the black chamber, thinking mostly about how much longer I might stand there before violence is done to etiquette or good breeding.

When I return to the courtyard or patio the table has been laid and all the adults are seated, except the grandparents, Cristian, who was up all night attending to the fallout of the Buruienești cloud rupture and is asleep in bed, and Elvira, who it seems increasingly likely has planned the whole party, bless her, in order to secure time alone with Sylvie.

I join the group and we eat from the platters of the pork belly, tenderloin, and flank heavily brined and smoked earlier in the afternoon; the meats are cold now, sliced thick, garnished with hard sharp red olives. Other plates hold varieties of the firm, salty, fresh Romanian cheeses, some of which have names such as *caș* or *cașcaval*, others which take only the general appellation of "cheese," *brânză*, and to my palate seem interchangeable but for slight variations in consistency or whiteness. There are finger bowls of coarse salt, baskets of soft bread that has been segmented by the crushing action of a dull knife.

Sliced tomatoes, sliced cucumbers, the whole green onions with plum-sized white bulbs consumed evidently with all proper meals as a kind of relish, the green portion being grasped and later discarded, as British miners of old are said to have discarded the smutted crust of the pasty, a meat pie whose format evolved in response to the miner's dirty hand, though I doubt such a story can be true. Another relish, an effete European chili varietal, is served with every soup, though at this meal no soup has appeared.

I eat heartily, to the point of my usual worry that I am attracting attention to myself, a worry I address probably counterproductively by offering the meat plate around the table. I doubt that manners here condone passing plates. This is much more a reaching culture, a franker culture.

Naturally there appears a second course. I am too full to partake of it without discomfort, though given the number of plates in service only a stupid person would have failed to anticipate it. *Sarmale*, the national dish: ground meat, salt, rice, bread, and chopped carrots, bundled in cabbage or grape leaves, served always with sour cream, *smântână*. This particular *smântână*, the sublimest dairy product I have encountered, is smooth, profoundly creamy, with a sourness so faint that it functions more as a question than as a characteristic, and a consistency almost like caramel or dulce de leche, forming of itself long, unbreakable strands between spoon and bowl.

When I see Bogdan spread this *smântână* on the coarse brown bread, I make a mental note to do the same as soon as a space clears on my plate, as soon as I have finished my *sarmale*, over which I am just now ladling a second coat of *smântână*, full though I am. I resolve again to give up dairy products, once I get back on track with my vegetarianism. The subtlest flavors, and in some cases therefore the most prized, are forms of doubt.

Ileana's phone rings. It is her husband, Ion, whose alcoholism seems openly to be regarded as an amusing quirk. Paula asks to be handed the phone so that she might play Ion the gentle trick of answering it in place of his wife. The group seems to approve the idea.

Ion needs to know, as Paula explains to me in real time, alternating between Romanian into the handset and English aside, where are the keys to his and Ileana's apartment in Roman, since he is locked out. His request makes no sense to me, unless he means a spare key concealed outside the building, a convention appropriate to village but not to city life. After a while Paula hands the phone back to Ileana, in whose efficient but not terse conversation with Ion I detect neither irritation nor shame. "My husband's weakness," the prose says.

Paula explains to me that last night Ion held a retirement party for himself, men only, and that that is why he has not attended the present function, the meat-smoking party. This is a second explanation that makes no sense to me. He's not entirely sober, Paula adds. The voices of my table companions grow muffled as I watch the bubbles stream in Bogdan's little glass of beer. Maybe I have given up drinking for no good reason.

This thought marks the entrance to one of the longer and more familiar numbers in my repertoire, a rumination which has the distinction of providing at certain turnings a sense of bittersweet pleasure, invoking as it does the comforts of home, the memory of various stages of intoxication and drunkenness. It begins typically with a procession through my immediate surroundings in the room in Topeka where I lie in my youth bed with a bottle of bourbon, having recurred yet again to the basement of my parents' house following a difficult breakup. It is the period in which I first have the sense of living for alcohol.

"Case bottle," the prose says, "first serious relationship." Folding table, computer, I set these up by the bookcase in the room and before lying down for the night I sit drinking Michelob and listening to a famous singer-songwriter's feel-good hit "Mexico" on repeat, a song chosen because this, my first serious relationship, has fallen apart in Mexico, and because in fact the first signs of trouble manifested at a wedding given at the singer-songwriter's house in Martha's Vineyard. "A brilliant match," the prose says, touching on my most secret self-laceration at the time. "My girlfriend at the time," it says, a phrase that feels like it issues from my neck.

Seated comfortably at the folding table I drink cold beer and delete lines of poetry from the Mexico notebook. The bourbon is my own stock, but the Michelob comes from a refrigerator in my parents' garage, beside a terrarium, still filled with cedar shavings, artifact of a previous minor depression.

But which, after all, did I not experience as "my first serious relationship"? Here the rumination telescopes, accelerates, as if rushing to get a story straight. As the summer of 1997 draws to a close, either because I have taken too much MDMA and perturbed my limbic system, or else because my heart is shortly to be, in a word, broken, by my girlfriend at the time, a junior at Sarah Lawrence, who sees, accurately, no reasonable way to prolong our summer romance—but that's not quite how it happens.

For a time I am just standing in the stairway outside the rooms at Caius College, where we have come for a poetry workshop, part of what is essentially a tourist program for American students. Study English at Cambridge, I recall the poster saying, though the academic credits were awarded by the University of New Hampshire. The marble treads hold deep concavities worn by a cultural process more time-honored, I tell myself, than any in my home country. Later I think of the Anasazi, though that is no longer the preferred term.

When the program comes to an end I realize definitively that I am in love, or maybe it would be more accurate to say that on the last day something in me gives and I resolve definitively to be in love, and in the stairwell as we draw out a long valedictory embrace I say as much, and she responds that she loves me, too, an intelligence I receive not with joy but with grave solemnity, fixing my gaze in the space in front of my chest and holding it there at all costs, as though to stabilize the expression on my face and in my voice, as though the slightest movement might upset a delicate emotional balance, causing me to express unseemly glee or burst into tears, demolishing our pact. The precise wording of her response is "Me, too."

I return from the poetry workshop and commence the fall semester of my biology studies at KU as the days wither and shrink. Mayfield, my favorite teacher, is just making himself comfortable, sitting in his fashion on the desktop, arms propped stiffly behind him. The room smells permanently of formaldehyde or a formaldehyde substitute. Today's focus is insect respiration, but he strays onto the topic of the book lung, feature of an adjacent class, Arachnida. I withdraw from school, move back for the first time into my parents' basement in Topeka, and take a job installing fiberglass insulation.

But first, or at any rate in October of that year, I drive all night and all day to the dorm room in Bronxville; it's the weeknight they refer to as "Thursday-night-all-night dance party," if Thursday is in fact the night. My girlfriend at the time, the first thing she does is take me to Jhonny's place, or just outside, where I sit in the car; I never learn his full name. I think of his last name as [sic], the ex-boyfriend about whom I have heard so much, drug dealer.

I wait in the car for an incredibly long time, two, then three hours, then four, the whole Funkmaster Flex radio show, then all of DJ Skribble's show. I tear up my throat and lungs smoking the rest of the Parliaments. She returns to the car. What did you get, I say. Oh, Cyrus, he didn't have anything, sorry. I'm not enjoying the sound of my name.

The party has vanished from memory. There is one part afterward where I return from the shower wrapped in a towel, having scrubbed myself as if for inspection, wantonly dispensing Victoria's Secret shampoo in the stall, where I can discover no soap. Rounding the corner into her room and facing the bed as I let the towel drop, I give a start. It takes me a moment to process the image, my girlfriend at the time having changed into gray sweatpants and hoodie, hood drawn tightly around the M38 gas mask strapped to her face, military surplus, a mask she does not remove as she explains to me, practically shouting, that she wears it to prevent the hoarseness and sore throat of an ecstasy hangover.

Can we still have sex, I ask in an uncharacteristically blunt way—at the time I think of it, charitably, as "animal-istic," a manner alien to me that in truth represents partly an unintelligible expression of anger or hurt feelings, and partly a panicked effort to act tough, since I feel I am going to begin crying at any moment, perhaps already have. No, Cyrus, she says, speaking now in baby talk, but with a strange booming quality because of the respirator.

Red acrylic bong, goes the rumination, little black mouse. It is my first season of staying high each waking hour, and it seems to me that the mouse represents not so much the effect of the depression as that of the period of adjustment in which my judgment does not function so reliably as it will, with occasional exceptions, during the next fifteen years of being high. But the mouse is also a symptom of the depression, for it is a sense of loneliness, or the panic brought on by the acuteness of the sense, that drives me to the pet store to purchase it, a tiny thing whose potential efficacy against loneliness is plainly zero or close to zero, the low expectations manifest in such a plan themselves classically symptomatic of depression.

There is an aspect, too, later to become all too familiar, of trying to cheer myself up by means which would have worked at one time, but only in childhood, for example a trip to the pet store, a place I now despise, though once I loved it better than a zoo. And what could make a young boy happier than to own a real gun.

I buy several packages of ten-inch flour tortillas, two large bags of shredded sharp cheddar cheese, six cans of refried beans, and two large bottles of Frank's RedHot, and after the first thirty minutes of wonder and exhilaration consequent to the bong hit, an interval I typically while away standing at the sliding door to the balcony or even sitting on the balcony on the east wall of my room, strange that I don't recall this more clearly or centrally, it seems like a great asset, something like that could make for a great year—what I remember is the excessive, ungainly height of the balcony rail, the absurd narrowness of the balcony floor, I can never find a comfortable way to sit there, plus in every memory I have of Kentucky Street it is raining, even though I recognize the chronic rain of recollection as a cliché—I lay down one tortilla, spread a half inch of refried beans, a half inch of shredded cheese, another tortilla, and more cheese, then microwave on high for three to five minutes. I like to nuke the quesadilla until the orange oil separates from the cheese and the milk solids harden into porous orange plaques.

Once the neighbor from next door comes over, a young man whose narrative is defined and dominated by the fact of his great love affair having ended, no one is sure how long ago. He is one of the few twenty-two-year-olds I know who admits to being depressed—this is toward the end of the twentieth century—he is about to drop out of the BFA program. At one point he develops pleurisy, probably from the terrible brick weed to which he enjoys unintermitted access. Years later, after I have been hired as assistant professor, the proudest professional achievement of my life, Paula and I visit a bad restaurant—every midwestern restaurant I've patronized is bad, but proportionally to its putting on of airs—and I recognize him as the waiter. I spend the celebratory meal failing to recall his name.

I notice as he sets down my black rectangular plate of vegetarian General Tso's chicken the broad studded leather wristbands, both wrists. When our check arrives there is a note in childlike hand on the receipt, good to see you again, if you ever want to hang out, my number is / Travis 785-383-4332.

One rainy afternoon, probably the last afternoon ever in the apartment, I spend hitting the bong and watching the mouse tremble in my cupped palm. After that it goes into the terrarium with the cedar shavings, the months' supply of water and food pellets, never again to roam, though it travels with me to Topeka, where, so caged, it abides on the dark shelf in the garage.

I change the water a couple of times and dump more food pellets into the maroon ramekin. I put a whole roll of toilet paper in the terrarium, a stoned idea but not a stupid one. The mouse shreds some of the paper and sleeps, so I believe, in a nest or bed constructed of this material inside the cardboard tube. As winter arrives I sometimes wonder if the mouse is cold. I glance at the dark shelf beside me when I open the refrigerator for beer.

Some winters later I retrieve another Michelob and try to remember when and how I disposed of the mouse's body, as I feel sure I must have done. Once more, I make the old effort to reassure myself that what the mouse really wanted, what it wanted most, was to be left alone, something doubtless true in its way. "Ten degrees of frost," the prose says. One night I leave the refrigerator door ajar and the beer freezes, splitting its fluted golden cans.

The rumination is at the point of my falling down in a crowded jetway as I attempt to board the plane—in youth and early adulthood I exhibit a tendency to fall in love with New Yorkers—that conducts me toward a weekend of sullen, futile negotiation or whatever it is with my girl-friend at the time, who stays that January in her mother's apartment on Park Avenue. I rise from the adult fall with a sudden clear determination never again to drink, a res-olution which appears fully formed and has remained intact these eleven years.

Twelve, thirteen. I rehearse the phrases that in the first weeks of sobriety hold special meaning for me, phrases about dedication and seriousness and my life's center, forms of focus which at the time I believe life has presented me with an opportunity to shift away from drinking and onto writing, or maybe it presents me with a choice, that I must focus exclusively on one or the other.

This term "sobriety" bothers me, since many years must pass before I can give up marijuana, the drug I love best of all, amid similar circumstances and with similar fanta-sies about getting serious, shifting focus, committing to the career of writer, though now there is a sense of it be-ing late to commit to any career. Certainly it is too late to move to New York. "Drugs are not symbolic," the prose says, quoting Duchamp, "but the addiction is similar. And that no doubt makes you waste a fantastic amount of time. That happened to me and probably helped me do what I wanted. Paint as little as possible and not repeat my paintings. It works out well. Chess fills your time when you don't paint."

Maybe I quit smoking pot for nothing. I have the sudden insight that at some point Travis has attempted to kill himself. "Consolations of hemp," the prose says.

I decline to help Paula finish her *sarmale*. When she sees me loading a slice of bread with *smântână* she says in Romanian, loudly and with a tone of pleasant mockery which the others receive with laughter, What, did you learn that from Bogdan? Ileana sounds like she's trying to close down the phone conversation with Ion.

Oh, he lied to me! Paula says suddenly. He's not outside the apartment trying to get in! He's inside the apartment trying to get out.

My daughter is making liberal use of a hand gesture, not a new one, in fact one of the first, actually the only one she has worthy of the name "gesture," but which, without outwardly changing, seems now to be undergoing expansion and refinement of meaning. Though she is left-handed, she makes it with either hand indifferently, and at first she seems simply to be pointing. However, she develops the gesture I think before her sensorium is nuanced enough to offer indicable or indexable points or objects of interest. Of course from early on she is capable of exhibiting, and what is probably the same thing, directing interest or attention. It is the concept of indication that she has not yet developed, though she seems to be developing it now; maybe its development and the gesture have been linked all along. At a glance she appears to be pointing, but if I look with any care at what she is doing I see it bears only the most superficial resemblance to pointing.

For example her finger, and it is her index finger, extends always in the same general direction, upward. Also, significantly, the finger is never in plane with her line of sight,

and not even parallel with the line of her forearm, but in-
clined from both.

My daughter employs her gesture always with a kind of
diligence or focus that marks off the gesture's time frame
and persists until her attention has migrated. But when
we arrive in Romania one week after her first birthday—at which point she can say clearly both "mama" and
"papa," clearly but without reference, sometimes saying
*mamamamamam* or *papapapapa* or even *mapa*—the gesture undergoes two further refinements that make these
speculations seem less relevant.

Firstly, she seems increasingly intent on scrutinizing or
watching the extended finger, and, perhaps to this end,
secondly, she introduces a degree of radial movement, so
that once she has, at arm's length, extended the finger—
watching, it seems to me carefully and judiciously, with
neither skepticism nor wonder—she gradually rotates her
wrist inward until the finger stands at about thirty degrees
to the horizontal. I assume this represents the range of
motion that is easy to her.

Degrees, minutes, and seconds—how young the concept
of a minute is, and how fitting that "second" should term
what it terms, the second of two diminutive additional
divisions made to a clock face that seemed complete to
begin with.

I have no theory of my daughter's gesture without situating it, that is without being able to say, if not why she does it, then at least when and where she does it, generally, and on this question it seems to me I have two lines of inquiry. The more robust proceeds from the idea that the gesture correlates to an increased awareness of surroundings as such, as opposed to what I imagine as the status quo ante, an infant sensorial oneness with surroundings, a state neither communicating with oblivion nor removed from it.

I call this an imagined status, but considering that the infant's material and developmental continuity with her surroundings is plain to see, since she starts out as an egg, a jolt of seed, from which, at various concentric radii, on shelves and trees or themselves in embryo the nutrients that substantiate her body stand some ways off, then it is more than imagination to see her awareness of an environment evolving ab ovo, just as the more fundamental distinction of her body from an environment is evolving ab ovo, out from a state of oneness with the universe later to be regarded as her environment.

The more I continue in this line, the more closely it seems connected to the second, fainter line of inquiry, that the child's performance of the gesture has, for me, the quality of solemn exhibition or demonstration. And at first, just as I have jumped to the conclusion that the finger points at something beyond, so I jump to the conclusion that the demonstration, if that's what it is, is performed for the benefit of onlookers, that is, Paula and me. But as I consider it more closely I feel less and less that it is a demonstration outward, and increasingly that it is a demonstration so fundamental that the gesture itself brings about the conditions necessary for its observation.

My daughter, by extending her finger, effectively distinguishes herself as a will and an observer, a distinction that entails the splitting off of a universe ulterior and in some senses opposed to this will. I imagine a cascade of subsidiary distinctions, such as the distinction of the hand from its owner, the finger from the hand, and so forth. I imagine her mentally pronouncing "peace be upon you," "I am the truth," something along those lines.

I am reminded of the gestural cliché in icon paintings, a gesture whose name or provenance I don't know, but which I have always assumed is a gesture of benediction, although it could be a kind of Abrahamic mudra, the hand is lax, the index finger extended upward, sometimes together with the middle and even the pinky finger—I wonder if "baby" is coming to replace "fetus" or "embryo" the same way "pinky" has supplanted any and all grown-up terms for the small finger, *digitus minimus manus*—and then the thumb sometimes binding the ring or ring and pinky fingers loosely.

I can't determine whether it has a name, although that it should lack one is inconceivable to me. Later it is suggested to me that the gesture has descended from a Roman one signifying address, address to a group, I assume, unlike the Clinton thumb, signifying address to an individual, and, in images of Christ Pantocrator, its typical context, evolved into a christogram, with the index, middle, ring/thumb, and pinky fingers respectively spelling out the letters *ICXC*, the first and last letters of the lunate sigmoid spelling of Christ's name.

I consider the Catholic devotion called the Little Sachet, a pouch holding a tiny folded paper bearing the christogram *JHS* and the so-called gospel of the circumcision. "And when eight days were completed for the circumcision of the Child," the prose supplies, "His name was called Jesus, the name given by the angel before He was conceived in the womb."

Or Pascal's tiny folded account, worn always in a little sachet on his person, of the car crash, the carriage accident, that precipitated his conversion and nearly claimed his life. Pascal in eight days of toothache contemplating the cycloid, the scalloped curve described by a point on a rolling wheel, "a such pleasant feeling." Pascal dead at thirty-nine, gastric carcinoma.

•

Paula remains very busy securing for Sylvia all rights and privileges of Romanian citizenship. She must get apostilles of marriage and birth certificate too, American documents, and this running around with her father, including a tense scene in Roman where, he being an official, they cut a day-old line, totally out of character for him, consumes much of the first week. Maybe Paula wants it to be consumed. As it happens her ID card has also expired. In the few minutes it takes us to fall asleep I try, in a loving way, to bring up the fact that we have not heard back from the laboratory about the fetal test results. We talk about the experience of waiting. I have no clear memory of talking about a plan.

In photographs elite chess players are often seen to be writing, possibly because in the tournaments where they congregate it has long been required that at the end of each turn the players record their moves on the slips of paper provided to them individually for that purpose, which they sign at the conclusion of the game.

In a preponderance of photographs, the most iconic, historic photographs, the great masters are seen not in the act of moving a piece, but in that of recording the move—e4, Nf3, Bb5, O-O—on this slip of paper which, incidentally, they are prohibited from marking in any other way, save for the signature. This moment between moves is understandably the apposite moment, the considerate moment in which to record an image.

The next time we are in the village it falls to me to put the baby to bed upstairs for a nap, a task during which I fall asleep next to her and am awoken by a vivid, prose-like dream. Because Sylvie is still asleep I lie in state on the bed, hands clasped over my chest. Through half-closed eyes I see Paula appear in the doorway, obviously unaware I am awake. She raises her phone, steadies it, snaps a photo, then turns and disappears from view.

As quietly as possible I slide out of the bed and sit on the floor to write down some expression of what seems to me, in my somnolence, the almost magical beauty, symmetry, and meaning inherent among these contingencies— the dream, the photo, the baby—and others I can no longer recall. But as soon as I get hold of my notebook Sylvie sits up, squints, and makes her gesture. By the time I have laid her back down to sleep, the sensation of meaning has vanished.

Underneath the indoor roller coaster, a structure which figures often, like the airplane and the sailing ship, in my dreams—I think such schemata arise from the kinesthetic confusion of the dreaming mind uncoupled from the body—there is cool golden sand, sculpted in the uncanny formations that underlie certain buildings and are representative not of natural erosive processes, but of a fossil-like record of a shelter's construction, men moving underneath the floor, and it occurs to me how strangely clean the space is, not least in light of the seediness and decrepitude of the dream carnival.

Beneath the ride I feel a potentiated version of the dread visited upon me each day of this trip, dread of illness, earthquake, choking, and car crash, on top of that, chauvinistic dread of superstitious or incompetent medical personnel, dread in this dream of failing to locate Sylvie, whom in a moment of incredible carelessness I have taken with me to ride the roller coaster, a ride whose rickety cars are in no way equipped to secure an infant—Sylvie of course, high on the driftwood track, has fallen out—far greater dread of encountering her remains, but there is nothing, only cool, crusty sand, shaped in the expression of its last disturbance, the welter of machines and workers who spread it there, or as a by-product of whose labor it appeared, untold years ago.

When my wandering has taken me a full circuit of this realm, a space full of the topological contradictions of dream, I see the coaster train parked at the deck-like boarding platform, where it was not earlier, when as preamble I partially destroyed this platform, with unreal strength first prising out by hand the long boards, their nails squealing and groaning, then splintering the wood in a misguided display of rage and, so it seemed to me, pride in my excessive strength and the virulence or virility of my anger. Even here, during this moment, I reflect that the behavior can bring about no good and will only reduce the speed and efficacy of my search, and I curse the weakness this display of power reveals, a childish and narcissistic submission to the low impulses of frustration and pride.

Again the prose I experienced in the company of the medical student and her father reappears, perhaps sardonically, since as I run clumsily to the assembly of small red cars the words that flash across my mind are "my heart leapt when I saw the train." But of course as I inspect them one by one, standing or floating impossibly in a spot that allows me a comprehensive overhead view, the cars, not the words, I realize that Sylvie will not be in any of them, not because this can be known, but because it is what I deserve, and I search the remaining cars only as an exercise in self-harm. Later I recall that the car seat, not the toddler one we've brought to Romania, but the infant one, red and too small, is the focus of our one big fight leading up to the trip.

Suddenly through the dimness of the cavernous space I see a skiff approaching, punted by a girl dressed as a carnival employee. Although the gravity of this situation is clear to me, I lose myself for a moment in meaningless speculation about whether a carnival employee might trust that her uniform has been laundered at any point in its transmission from previous owner to herself. This musing—which recalls to me the discomfort of trying to sleep in skeevy locales—brings on more curses, since I indulge in it, to dire loss of time and industry, primarily as a way of admiring the novelty or ingenuity of my own imagination, even though I have a compelling suspicion that this idea specifically, and in fact my imagination as a whole, lacks novelty and ingenuity.

Despite myself I recall the Super 8 in Cheyenne, where, when I lie down on the clean white sheets, wetness transpires from the mattress soaked with I know not what, leaving a dark spot in the shape of my body, like the Turin shroud.

For a moment the child employee and the skiff form a tableau vivant of Arnold Böcklin's *Isle of the Dead*, and once more, wasting irreplaceable time, I pause to congratulate myself for recognizing the similarity and for knowing the name of the artist and the work, a painting Böcklin apparently reproduced numerous times in fulfillment of social or financial obligations.

I see, as expected, the red bundle of the car seat and, as it draws periodically closer, a figure representing the superposition of Sylvie live and dead. By this I understand the dream to be offering me a choice between overwhelming relief and its antithesis, and without making any decision of which I am aware, I sweep the child into my arms and run, "sobbing with joy," back in the direction of the house, which stands on or adjacent to the carnival grounds. There is a door leading from the shadowy arena of the roller coaster into the house's main room. As I cross the boarding platform I pass a mounded puddle of vomit, fresh vomit, and seeing it makes me vomit, right away, and the prose flashes again before my eyes, "pure emotion."

Despite my "tear-stained face" I assume an air of stupid nonchalance as I cross the threshold of the house, Paula's house in the village. On the sofa sits my brother with a man inexplicably known to me as "David," nominally my brother's friend from the math department, but, as is obvious in retrospect, actually a fifteen-years-aged version of my brother himself.

What is my brother doing here, the prose says, merging with my thoughts and then with the voice of David. He's *still* here, David corrects me irritably. "Drinking nervously," David adds, unironically, except the prose has scare quotes, and, despite the fact that the situation seems to be one of urgent tension, I allow myself one more moment of smugness, silently observing that one recognizes the "scare" in "scare quotes" as the one in "scarecrow," a special sense of "scare" that indicates lack of substance, as if to enclose an argument in scare quotes was to generate a straw man.

"Swelling with arrogant pride" I turn to face David down, but at that moment I see that he is right, that my brother has obviously been here from the beginning of the dream. David has arrived with a bottle of Dewar's and one of Johnnie Walker, plus a store of wry remarks I find a little distasteful. He tells a joke about the university president's complaint to the dean of the school of medicine about the need for expensive research equipment. Why can't you be more like the mathematicians? All they need is paper, pencils, and wastebaskets.

What about the philosophers, replies the physician. They require only paper and pencils. Then it strikes me that David is not fifteen years older than my brother, but twelve years older, precisely the duration, if you count his master's, of my brother's enrollment in the PhD program thus far. Later Ben observes that this episode recalls Kafka's "The Judgment." David is of course my father's name.

•

We are on our way back from seeing the priest and I am trying, wedged in the back of the Opel, to convince myself that given the extent of my involvement with the church, an entanglement complicated considerably by this morning's meeting, my most righteous tactic would not be to deny Paula any chance to translate what the priest has said over the course of an hour in a room of uncertain purpose, like a budget psychiatrist's office, except with votive candles and a crown of real thorns, locust thorns, colorful synthetic throws shrouding the chairs, printed with low-definition floral designs.

As it stands I know only that the expensive and elaborate ceremony Paula's family has striven to arrange for us in Sighișoara and which we have already once failed to attend, in the year of its first being scheduled, owing to another significant failure of time management, a procrastination preventing Paula from getting the requisite visa in time, so now, two years hence, the Sighișoara hotel still has Paula's parents' cash deposit—I know only that we still plan to drive there, and that the event has changed from wedding party to some other ceremony, a Catholic ceremony whose principal participant is Sylvie, a baptism or confirmation or, I guess, some formal presentation of the child to her godparents, Corina and Doru. If I learn no more I can perform the dumb show of whatever ritual the church requires of me, the father, and this, or so I am trying to convince myself, leaves me on higher ground than if I take part in the ceremony with fuller comprehension of its transcript.

The priest's meeting room is in a building, maybe his domicile, across the street from a large orange church constructed according to what I want to call futurist principles and designed, I guess, to resemble the prow of a great ark. As we wait to be let in, the priest fumbling on the other side of a characteristically temperamental dead bolt of local make, in its tolerances so unlike the Yale lock, I think of Father Mapple's noble sermon, his chapel which looks like a ship's cabin, and of Ishmael kneeling to Queequeg's black idol, Yojo, a figure I sometimes refer to, to the amusement of my students, as #Yolo. I wonder if they know the joke is scripted.

The air of resignation to appear cheerful is not the same thing as a cheerful air, but is the air with which the priest inaugurates his twenty minutes of small talk. Gradually I recall that this priest is the same who, together with some kind of assistant—not the *sora* or sister-cohabitant of the village priests, but a stocky young man dressed for business—was summoned to the apartment one winter we were in Roman, for what I understood to be a sort of annual house-blessing; I was struck then as now by the same dutiful dispensation of small talk, as we, the priest, and the unacknowledged man I think of privately as the priest's "muscle," maybe "factotum" is better, exchanged tight-lipped smiles in the living room. Come in, be seated, twenty minutes of small talk, presentation of goods, discreet exchange for cash, leave-taking, just like a friendly drug deal, down to the folded banknotes pressed as if neither party were seeing it happen into the priest's palm.

Though no money changes hands on the present occasion, in character and duration the small talk is the same. I comprehend about half of it, which means following it thematically, but being mostly in the dark as to what claims or propositions are made, or whether their relationship to content is affirmative or negative. I understand that the priest is making a paternalistic comment about Paula's changed appearance, she replies yes, that she's gained fifteen kilos, then the priest pauses expectantly. "Pursing his plump lips," the prose says.

After a moment, smoothing his trousers in a gesture of complacent self-appraisal, the priest announces that his appearance, too, has changed. For he has lost eleven kilos, and hopes to continue losing kilos until the tally reaches a word I recognize as numerical but which I can't mentally retain long enough to sort. The word has existed like a friend's face seen on the street, without realizing one has seen it, so that a few moments later, when with seemingly random intentness you peer at a stranger's face, the friend comes to mind, in fact you mistake the stranger for the friend. That I should hear a word clearly but lose track of its sound before it can be formalized is a possibility which, to my further distraction, I consider now for the first time.

It is often the case that when I mistake a stranger for some friend, however long it's been, the friend materializes. Synchronicity or the Baader-Meinhof phenomenon or whatever it is, the more general effect in question, maybe it's the fact that the number of words or concepts to which we are exposed in a given moment exceeds, by orders of magnitude, those we can put to use. But the stream of unnoticed meanings rushing by must leave its impression, carving a channel for insights of the form "incredible, but I learned this word only yesterday." Yesterday's encounter does not sensibly exist, but is pulled up into the status of conscious experience only by the shock of today's recognition, so that encountering the word today, and encountering it yesterday, are in some meaningful way simultaneous.

It is with the same simultaneity that I generally experience dreams, not as a duration in sleep, certainly not as a chain of events, but rather, at the moment of waking, as an instantaneous precipitation or concatenation of images, memories in the sense that all representations are memories, residues salvaged from the flood of time and, by juxtaposition alone, endowed with narrative coherence and meaning. The dream comes into being at once, outside of time, as a constellation of previously unlinked events, eventualities. Only on waking—though since it is made from memories, it is experienced as one—do I perceive the dream narrative: that I have been in such a place, that Paula was there, and Zhutchka, my dog who died.

We congratulate the priest on his loss. Gabriela, who seems to have genuine rapport with him, asks how he's done it. Taking a breath and airing the first words of the sentence as though delivering himself of a long-held secret, he utters a series of unintelligible phrases ending with the trade name for a pyramidally marketed range of dietary supplements, "Herbalife."

As he speaks, I watch his shoes, a characteristically European type of sandal, one I believe to have evolved—perhaps through hybridization with the leather walking or touring shoe—from the white-water rafting sandal with which in the mid-1980s the American company Teva saw explosive success. The priest's sandals have no recognizable brand; like all footwear here, they look inexpensive to me. I wonder if Americans are especially sensitive to the market value of clothing, footwear, and accessories.

Certainly this is the cardinal form of judgment in the American milieu of adolescence, a social period experienced as pure, meaningless hierarchization, and whose boundary with later life is increasingly harder to locate.

There is a kind of maturity in which instead of evaluating appearances according to price, one evaluates them in terms of taste, a quantity perhaps more mysterious than money, but acquired by the same prerogative. I sometimes feel that becoming a father absolves me of certain responsibilities to taste. Two days ago at the ATM on Roman's main street I was wearing my own rafting-type sandals, Chaco, a brand even more expensive than Teva and frankly a better article, when an aggressive shortchange artist tried to engage me.

Paula turns to me and says, did you understand all that, and I answer, yes, naturally, I have understood some, except I don't know how to say some, don't know whether the noun meaning "some" differs from the indefinite article, "some trees," so instead I say, "naturally, I have understood a little" or perhaps "I have understood little." Then, to demonstrate, and since I recall the priest having mentioned exercise, the Romanian phrasal verb for which is *a face sport*, I address him, "what sport you make," a contribution resulting in silence during which embarrassment is shared among Paula, Gabriela, and the priest, who takes the lion's share. With a summary motion of his hand he proceeds, holding forth for twenty-five minutes or so on our business matter. I hear my name and Paula's, as well as some nouns repeated over and over, apparently cognate with contraception, abortion, procreation, and sin. At one point he seems to say, for reproduction is good, but for relaxation is a sin, an epigram which strikes me as authentically celibate, and my respect for him rises slightly. Just once do I hear the word for god, a word not easy to miss, *dumnezeu*.

I feel my eyes move, locking my gaze up and a little bit to the side in a way that suggests lostness in thought; I have read that this pensive gaze even indicates by its direction what part of the brain one is lost in, what piece of the mind. It is the grayscale b-mode image of my son, his figure, maybe it is more abstraction than figure, a shifting cross section produced as the technician slides her transducer over sound-conducting gel scooped from a special warming vessel and spread across the globe of Paula's abdomen.

Sonography, of course, is an image of delay, building up its sandy portraits by counting the moments it takes for an echo to return to its source, visualizing this latency as longitudinal distance, visualizing the echo's strength as brightness. The echoes themselves occur when the sound reaches boundaries in the body.

Impediment that it is, the echogenic focus in my son's heart brightens and fades, coming in and out of view as

the technician worries it with her transducer. Her persev-
eration reminds me of the way a searcher sweeps a visual
field, slowing or arresting the progress of her gaze again
and again at the same spot, as if there existed a distinction
between finding the hiding place and finding what is
hidden. The object of a search must end the search, but
this item or point of interest only intensifies and prolongs
it. What is it she sees or does not see?

I believe the priest is trying to shame or intimidate my wife
by cataloging the sexual and reproductive prohibitions of
the church, a litany which, if I may say so, we have violated
exhaustively, and I glare at his sandals, looking up from
time to time to glare at his face, at least it feels like glar-
ing to me, objectively speaking I doubt it appears all that
tough; I probably look more like a suitor holding in a fart.

Then I realize, or so it seems, that his shaming of Paula
is only incidental to the matter, namely what needs to be
done with me in order for me to be considered fit to take
part. Like pins in the tumbler of a lock, five or six variables
sink into place. I will be required to pledge myself against
fornication and abortion, and recite additional phrases.
Then I perceive, to my dismay, that the priest is laying
out a schedule for the most rapid practicable conversion of
me, the child's father, to the Catholic faith.

There arises the anxiety symptom where I notice my
shirt beating visibly over the region of my heart and I fear

that others will notice it as well. However little I have seen them coming, I am rapidly meeting the conditions under which I must make some sort of fatal stand. On a vague imaginary chart, either a family tree or a map of Europe, I tally, in the form of estranged family members and alienated social groups, the losses I can expect to sustain. Panicking, I grope for some way to resolve the conflict.

This is not about you personally, I talk myself down. It is not about honor or truth. You are required to participate pro forma in a ritual that enacts the real function of establishing and solidifying social and familial relations around your daughter one year old. I think again about Ishmael and #Yolo, and about Father Mapple's noble sermon, organized around the metaphor of life as navigation, the cleric's role not as captain but as pilot, pilot in the nautical sense.

At present the Christian church represents perhaps the second-most grievously misinformed community of people in the world, I think. Of course humanity suffers countless misapprehensions more extravagant than theirs, but few more destructive in the realm of policy. Can I not find in myself some sympathy with them? But as the priest "drones on" (the prose), these efforts to shore up my peacemaking resources devolve into musing upon the handful of novels I have read closely, Pierre Bezuhov and his entry into the faithless chamber of commerce representing the Freemasons, how they lead him blindfolded through an initiation rite worthy of a modern-day frat house, whose climax I recall, perhaps inaccurately, to be that Pierre must announce, in the full company of masons, his greatest moral failing.

I imagine myself naked or partially clothed in a torchlit room, though as I import these details I become increasingly doubtful of my recollection of the Tolstoy. I look up from the blood the priest has, with a ceremonial saber, drawn on my fat, bare chest, and I whisper, "I . . . I started eating meat." But I can't seem to withdraw further into this fantasy, addressing for example the question of whether eating meat is really my greatest moral failing—certainly this is the spirit in which my imagination has offered it—or whether, as its parallelism to Pierre's claim of womanizing suggests, it is significant precisely because it is an expedient reply to a question whose true answer, could Pierre speak it, would obviate all the masonic bullshit and bring to a conclusion the whole ordeal of spiritual seeking. Later, to my horror, reading Troyat's biography, it seems to me Tolstoy's life is a crime against women.

I find myself thinking about the cliché of the contemporary job interview, "what would you say is your greatest weakness," whose practical function is to assess the applicant's talent for dissimulation, particularly in the suppression of inconvenient news. But I get no further into these questions—is Pierre right, in a way, since his betrothal to Ellen is actually the moment he drowns his conscience?—because the reverie switches texts, now it's *Charterhouse of Parma*. Julian Sobel, that's not his name, takes a long time to accept that the siphoning noises and the little splashes of earth all around him signify flying bullets. I see myself in a stubble field where projectiles continually raise puffs of dusty soil. Has it begun then? Am I really to convert to Catholicism, I, who everyone agrees is so pure of heart? I, with my reverence for the meanings of words?

I glare again at the buffed toenails set like semiprecious stones in the priest's cadaverous feet. Of course the more relevant precedent would be the sandal developed in the mid-1960s by a German, Karl Birkenstock. Paula addresses me for what I sense is a second time. Well?

My glare is less justified than I think, since, as Paula tells me that night in bed, the priest is explaining only that because her first marriage took place in the Orthodox Church, she is on the outs with the Catholics, and that in order to clear the way for whatever bureaucratic process lies ahead—the process we have come here to arrange, and of whose particulars I am even more uninformed than I hoped, since it is not any sort of rite for Sylvie, but in fact a wedding, a marriage ceremony for me and Paula— in order to clear the way for this process it is technically necessary for Paula to attend confession. To reduce the awkwardness of the procedure she should review the key behavioral constraints of the church, all of which at present concern themselves with reproduction and sexual intercourse. Apparently the priest explains this with subdued, affable irony. Yet the next day on the phone he flatly refuses to have anything more to do with her.

•

It seems to me that after some interval in Romania I lose access to my surroundings, immediate access, an immediacy I associate as general effect with processes such as travel and intoxication, or, to a lesser extent, concentration and meditation.

I dawdle about the grounds of some monastery, church, cultural center, and, as I discover, excellent restaurant on the scenic outskirts of Roman. The prose is saying something like "Make-A-Wish Foundation Denies Request for Unlimited Access to Pain Medication," which at first I see as a kind of headline, then as an aphorism, but later as a concise program for some work of fiction, especially as I have considered this foundation, about which I know little or nothing, to function primarily as a narrative enterprise, an institution whose products or works consist of stories generated for the benefit of prospective donors and, to a much lesser extent, that of the surviving family members of its deceased honorees, recipients, in every case I have heard of, of packages indistinguishable from those awarded with similar fanfare by game shows and radio contests, all-inclusive trips and cruises, or meetings and autographs, meals with a celebrity.

I wonder what it does to the souls of children, prompted to choose what in all the world they most desire, to experience the radical insufficiency of the world's offerings. When I reach the grassy gravel of the church parking lot, two children come to me, chanting supplications that end in a word for bread.

I hear fragments of the church service in a male voice amplified by what sounds like a megaphone. I'm sorry, I tell the children, I still don't understand Romanian. Money, money, money! the girl shouts, grinning. Money! shouts the boy, a moment later, a delay that suggests he is her younger sibling. Haven't got, I announce. The children skip or run away. I have the feeling that Sunday in this church parking lot surrounded by woods, fountains, gardens, beehives, and ponds is the highlight of their week.

The children pass me again, this time led by, of all people, Bogdan, who is explaining something to a woman with babe in arms, probably their mother. I hear the characteristic solenoid sound as he unlocks the car remotely to retrieve, with a cheerful, almost exuberant smile, two individually wrapped servings of crackers. The mother accepts these impassively, looking at Bogdan, not at the crackers, which she hands to the two already departing children. Paula is calling me from across the lawn.

I stick to the grass while Bogdan walks the gravel road—a needless risk, I feel—but we both make it to the especially nice terrace built onto the side of one of the larger and more recent buildings, one Elvira informs me was a sort of mansion before the communists seized the property and turned it into a school. There follows a discussion about which of the twelve or so tastefully laid tables for six is the nicest, a question whose clear answer seems to me, as I try to indicate, the one in back. I point out the bright translucent fiberglass composite roof slanting over the length of the terrace, the dark circle of shade lent by an oak sixty or eighty years old, whose acorns with a pleasant rapping sound drop periodically on the composite. When we get to the table so neatly accommodated by this shade we find it marked *rezervat*, and I feel a rush of anger, but the reservation turns out to be our own.

The excellent lunch—thin soup, hot rolls, baked turkey with green beans, the turkey dressed with tomatoes and capers and the green beans abundant with green garlic—tastes as though it has all issued, and I believe it has, from the various gardens and enclosures on site. There is a server who strikes me as a type, a person sixteen or seventeen years old whose effusion of love and admiration for my child betokens irrepressible happiness, a mood or manner constitutional with her, but that will stand as her default mode only for these two or three years of life. By the time she is twenty, any number of things will have compelled her to some alternative. She lifts up Sylvie and twirls with her, taking no notice of the baby's bewilderment, maybe because they cling to each other so tightly.

*Să vă trăiască*, the server entreats me—I am surprised to see her eyes filling with tears—*să vă trăiască*. I do my best, uncomprehendingly, to smile. Later I repeat the phrase to Paula, who says it is a conventional expression translatable as "may she live."

•

I listen to the electric streetcars, the noise of their motors higher and smoother than that of combustion engines, as we enter a long stairwell leading to the penthouse apartment in Iași that belongs to Alice and George, names I hesitate to speak, being forever of two minds how to pronounce them. I have looked forward to seeing this family, especially their two young daughters, but no sooner than I walk through the door do I find the air of the home charged with pervasive, unspoken strife. It is the third day of the rigorous three-day exam whose outcome is George's promotion from otorhinolaryngologist to primary doctor, the highest rank in a professional system whose tiers are obscure to me.

Congratulations, I say to him, loud and slow, on becoming primate. But George seems neither happy nor relieved. The wrinkles around his eyes put me in mind of the illustrations of Charles Schulz, the way Charlie Brown's face looks amid the distress that dogs his steps, sometimes in the form of a personal thunderhead. I grimace, recalling how, in my first volume of poems, I misspell Schulz's name.

George absents himself to one of the apartment's six balconies and I smell tobacco smoke. He is the only Romanian I know who seeks regular cardiovascular exercise, the only one who provisions car seats for his young children, so even when he reappears and then leaves again twenty minutes later and I smell the smoke again, I can hardly believe he is behind it. But that evening as we lounge on the nearby terrace of an upscale mall, he produces a pack of Winston cigarettes. Women's cigarettes, I think automatically, since they are white and extremely slender, like Virginia Slims, introduced in 1968 by Philip Morris and marketed exclusively to women, or the even slimmer Capri brand, brought out nearly two decades later, I am curious about that, by R.J. Reynolds. He smokes them right in front of the children, without apparent shame, though without show.

I think about how from here I can see, or would be able to see if I knew where to look, the apartment in which Paula and her first husband, whose name I have not taken especial care to learn, owned a floor, an apartment Paula's parents paid for and which she by verbal agreement during the divorce relinquished to him. The development of the mall complex in which we are sitting might have doubled or tripled the value of such an apartment, I think. I remember when Paula and I first met—we met, moved in together, married, and twice conceived in the space of three years—how I felt I had to keep after her about getting a divorce, a step whose importance she understood but which, for reasons that didn't matter to me at the time, whatever they were, she seemed to procrastinate. I wonder if this is not, in disguise, another penalty of my procrastination and the procrastination of the procrastinator mate I have sought out, a person I loved basically at first sight and from whom I will never part, that we do not now own a nice, and getting nicer by the minute, apartment in our favorite Romanian city.

The second night in Iași we go to Casa Vânatorului, a terrace restaurant in the city's principal park, to meet with Paula's former colleagues from the high school, and their spouses, everyone loves her. I believe she taught in Iași from 2000 to 2005, the chapter of her life before she moved to Emporia to do an MA. Casa Vânatorului must mean "house of the hunter" or "hunter's cabin" or perhaps "hunter house."

The park hosts the fittest stray dogs in the city, fittest in the ecological sense, and every time I visit there are plenty of people, young and old, walking wide paths of brick or stone. The terrain is mostly paved, with islands or isthmuses of chestnuts rising from thin lawns. There are elaborate playgrounds for children of various ages. Vendors of cotton candy, popcorn, and ice cream work from stalls or carts. I see two boys of about nine and twelve, first shouting at the parents of a girl about their age who is posing for a photograph, then at one of the gates to the terraces of Casa Vânatorului, where a waiter issues them terse instructions or some sort of rebuke. How I know at a glance that the park is a means of survival to them is hard to say. Their skin is darker, maybe that is the main thing, though I don't know if that marks them as pertaining to the other side of the only Romanian ethnic divide visible to me, that between people for whom the only available term is "Romanians," and the Romani underclass, people for whom the Romanian word is *țigan*, from Greek *Αθίγγανος*, said to mean "untouchable." Their own word, of obscure origin, for a member of the outgroup is *gadjo*.

Or maybe the more telling sign, among others—they are thin, sockless, their shorts and T-shirts are tiny on them— is their bearing in the presence of adults, whom they seem to regard not as parent figures, but rather as an untrustworthy, potentially dangerous species. It isn't lack of respect that the boys show, for example, to the parents for whose camera the girl has been posing, but rather respect of the kind shown a gun or wild animal, and their manner is pitched, successfully, at intimidation. Their boldness is authentic. It affects me to see two adults quail at the shaken fist of a twenty-kilo boy. With the waiter who instructs or reproaches them they adopt a slightly different manner, like the tone you take with representatives of a hated institution who may or may not personally deserve your rage but whom there exists no strategically sound reason to offend. "Socklessness," the prose says, "cousin of shoelessness."

The waiter, for his part, assumes a sternness that seems to overlie neither animus nor compassion. *Gata*, he keeps saying, which can mean "ready," "finished," or "enough," and in this context clearly enough means "move along now."

Doru, probably the alpha male and certainly the figure-head of our assembly, uses the same term in the same way when at the long table a thin voice sounds behind me, that of a boy twelve or thirteen. I think it best not to turn around. Paula and I have seated ourselves among her former colleagues. The wives drink lemonade and the husbands drink beer, a division observed in Romania due, I believe, in part to the strong consensus against drinking and driving. The voice is an excessively, affect-edly, I think, miserable one. But Doru, a man brimming with equal parts machismo and bonhomie, flicks or waves his hand and says, *hai, gata, gata.*

I feel not only that the stiffness of my posture is highly visible, but that I am imposing it on the other guests, flaunting my awkward stillness, if that makes sense, in their faces until they can focus on nothing else. The voice sounds again. It seems to me like the voice of a second-rate actor whose foot is caught, for the purposes of the scene, in a bear trap. Doru opens his billfold. Moving only my eyes I see him withdraw, from among notes of many de-nominations, several singles, single lei, each worth roughly thirty American cents. He seems also to be weighing the possibility of adding a ten or twenty or fifty, though his hand moves too fast now for me to learn how this uncertainty is resolved. *Gata*, he says with finality, giving the money, now get out of here.

Later Doru addresses a couple of remarks to the group about my teetotaling, as he did at our last gathering and has done, in fact, at every gathering we have attended. Mineral water! he says loudly, pounding his chest with one hand. Gives a man strength! With mineral water you'll grow a real *burta*, he says, referring to the protrusive omental fat, firm and carried high on the frame, in which particular form—the so-called beer belly—it is more prominent among this nation's men than any I have seen, and which American doctors say forebodes cardiac event.

During the meal Doru orders several rounds of beer for the table, the men of the table, as if they are not drinking fast enough. Denis, he shouts. Doru is the type to call a waiter by his first name, a slightly different type here than in the United States, since Romanian waiters are not subject to the ignominy of name tags or ritual verbal self-identification, Hi, my name is Travis and I'll be taking care of you tonight, and so forth. If Doru calls you Denis, it means he's asked you your name.

And bring another mineral water here, he shouts, having noticed as he unerringly does the precise moment I empty my bottle. His attentiveness plays a decisive role in winning me over to Doru. I think he wins me over. He is a type not easy to like, though equally difficult to dislike. As before, I find myself drinking many bottles of mineral water, absurdly many. Four liters of mineral water, as if this could impress anyone, let alone Doru. Strong! he laughs, girding my upper arm in his hand. Strong! he re-asserts, as if itemizing a long-term goal.

Looking away, he moves his hand to rest on the newer part of my body I recognize as "love handles," something I have developed since the knee injury shut down my running. I don't know whether to feel more ashamed of the flabbiness here or of that in my triceps, but with laying on of hands in these two locations, "strategic locations," the prose says, Doru establishes more or less complete dominance. How could I possibly compete, I think suddenly, with a husband named Dragos.

I also notice the level in a drinking glass. For some drinkers any assemblage of vessels functions sadly as a timepiece, one requiring consultation for clearance to order the next drink. I don't know if Doru is primarily a drinker, or just a considerate and highly sensitive observer, but he is my godparent, which, apart from spouse, is the most important social role conferred by Romanian marriage, and it is important that we like each other. "Clepsy-dra," the prose says. "Little hand."

Shortly after the beggar disappears another shows up. I see her clearly, a thin child of about eight who wears a clean white blouse and a white ribbon in her hair, as though the occasion demands it. She wants only food, and Doru—how do the children know, just as the waiters know, to approach Doru and not any of the other sixteen people here—Doru gives her from the closest of several heaping bowls a double handful of cherries, the national fruit. The girl recedes and I watch her thread a path to the waiters' beverage station set up against the iron fence enclosing the terrace. I am surprised to see appearing through the bars two sets of cupped hands—the two boys'. I want to know what system allows these people amicably to share the terrace; the first beggar, for example, clearly must visit the table prior to the girl in white, if he is to find there a soft touch.

•

On my last morning in Iași I drink too much coffee and am outraged as I sit on the toilet, thinking, with real conviction, such thoughts as that the Romanian tongue manages expressions of comparative quantity with, so it seems, an absurd set of constructions literally equivalent to "more many" and "more fewer." It renders "turtle," Paula insists, as "helmet frog." But before the caffeine rush is spent my anger subsides and I employ what remains of the high exploring the increasingly interesting question of George and Alice's marriage imploding.

The essence of welcome is in the show of welcome, I guess, and visible in the welcome George and Alice show us is an effort to conceal some awful disturbance in the relationship. There is also the matter of their appearing ancient to me, although we are the same age, at least that's what Paula says when I ask, and even more fascinating the matter of George's smoking. But most fascinating of all is the matter of his hand. It is made known, I don't recall how, that George is scheduled for surgery within the next few days to remove two screws from the proximal phalanx of his left index finger. Paula says Alice has indicated to her the presence of "a major relationship problem." I ask her how George broke the finger and she tells me she hasn't asked. We go on whispering for some time.

I am not very surprised when, on the way to the party at Casa Vânatorului, to which George is giving me a ride since Paula, Alice, and the children have filled the other car—George isn't attending the party because, strangely, he has plans to play tennis—he holds up his hand for me to see the long spiral scar of the incision made to insert the screws. I think it is apropos of a conversation we are having about not exercising as much as we'd like to, barriers to physical exercise, cares of a family man, that he raises the hand. When *this* happened, he says, showing me first the palm side, then the back, I couldn't play tennis or do my tractions. "Tractions" is a solecism I associate with the piece of fitness equipment in his study, a "chest expander" constructed from three long coil springs connecting two D-shaped handles.

To my eye, the chest expander is comically dated. In fact I recognize it only on the basis of having seen something like it represented in Warner Bros. cartoons, the most authoritative repository of clichés in the industrialized world, which normally depict the device in reference to a prewar formula of masculinity involving, for example, the black-and-white magazine advertisement targeting men insecure about being too skinny. Possibly it involves a picture of a swarthy, barrel-chested fellow in bathing trunks who kicks sand at a beachgoing couple. "Ninety-eight-pound weakling," the prose says. My knee, I think, wincing.

•

I assume the orthopedist, a man with the unusual name of Abner Meriwether, is going to be West African, but "Meriwether" turns out to be Irish, and "Abner" a given name popular in the Deep South. It takes about twenty minutes for him to appear in the consultation room. The end table is strewn with issues of *FLYING* and other magazines marketed to hobbyist pilots.

As I read I think about the annual subscription drives Whitson Elementary held to raise funds—funds for what I had no clear idea—which for me always ended with my mom purchasing two or three subscriptions in my name. Though I chose the magazines carefully, *Bicycling, Mountain Biking, Mountain Bike Action*, what motivated me were the trinkets and prizes awarded according to sales quota. Ghetto blaster, 44,850 points. I imagine myself or some other family man making the median Kansas City income—maybe a man of limited intellect or prone to sentimentality, a very high man—subscribing to *FLYING*.

Maybe I quit using drugs for nothing, I think. It's not like I have ever lost anything important because of my habits. I am not a real addict in that sense, not unless I am in some kind of denial. "His potential," the prose says.

Meriwether comes in wearing close-fitting slacks and cashmere sweater. Cyrus Console-Şoican, he says, that's quite a name. His manner involves pacing the consultation room briskly, gesturing with his hands as he prognosticates through a series of rhetorical questions. I like him. We talk about "staying active." He is a big believer in staying active. He gets it. Does he still play racquetball? Yes, because he loves the game. Does he pay the price? Every time. Does he take lots of ibuprofen? Vitamin I. Would he be delighted to open up the knee and reconstruct? Absolutely. Would it help? Not in the least.

I was disappointed in my physical therapist, I say. Meriwether looks at me with interest. Why? Well, I expected a concrete plan about how to get running again. I would say things like so what is the best way for me to start running again. Everybody's different, she would say. Can I set a goal of running daily again at some point? That depends on how soon you want to replace the knee, she would say. I tell Meriwether, I'm not totally sure why—actually the whole episode of taking him into my confidence about the PT is already embarrassing to me—that "her affect seemed depressed to me." She didn't seem to have any information for me. Well, says Meriwether, everybody is different.

I say to myself then that the PT and Meriwether are telling me basically the same thing, the truth. Your body wears out. The fuck did you expect. For the first time, the knee issue seems not only clear, but simple. What the professionals are telling me—whether or not they think of it in these terms explicitly—is that age, weakness, and death are not things held by the future, as I have always unquestioningly assumed, but are instead the very substance of the now.

How much of what I cling to as "my plan"—the idea of a routine that, vigilantly prosecuted, forever ensures my sobriety, health, happiness, well-being—has depended on the daily run? And how much time and energy have I invested, on a daily basis, in mentally cherishing the plan? Has it not been my chief source of security and comfort ever since I quit smoking pot, five years now? Six, seven?

My wife is a PT, Meriwether says.

•

In no other field does hesitation figure so centrally. "Defending champion Karjakin seemed to be the better prepared player as he blitzed his first 11 moves," the sportswriter says, "while Caruana stopped for a seven minutes think on his 10th move, and then thought for 23 minutes on 11.Be3."

Finally I ask George—I've been waiting two days for an opportunity—how he broke the finger and he replies, in uncharacteristically fluent, idiomatic English, "It's kind of a long story." "Prepared statement," the prose says.

I try to pinpoint the air of hopeful finality in this practiced, I think, response—it is faint enough that I take a moment to admire myself for noting it and for moving wisely and deftly on to the topic of which forms of exercise I like best, trail running, were it not for the goddamned knee—an astuteness basically continuous with what I secretly believe to be my exceptional perspicacity as a reader, something I doubt George has the means to appreciate.

That is, George believes his tactic has actually neutralized my desire to know how the finger was broken, since how could a person foresee any benefit in persisting with such curiosity, given that the story necessary to its satisfaction would require the effort of sustained, careful attention. I believe George suffers from inflated confidence in both his powers of explanation and his skill in devising expedients, solutions to complex, unique problems, a trait I associate with physicians.

I think about the colectivo driver in Tuxtla Gutiérrez—how he extends the stump of his left pinky, wrapped in a gauze bandage that is like a Warner Bros. cartoon version of a bandage, gingerly where his hand rests atop the steering wheel—and the few other injuries I've seen that something told me not to ask about, one of my best students, who shows up to class with weeping abrasions on her elbows and knees. "Stump," a term for which the amputee community seeks an alternative, for example "residual limb."

I look at George's hand again and hold up my own in the established way, turning both sides to him so he can see the scars of the crush wound I received in 1989 by meshing my fingers in the gears of an antique cider press. He looks politely in a way that gives me the impression he does not see the scars.

George, his colleague Sebastian, and I decide to bicycle sixty kilometers through the villages and beech forest outside of Iași, a kind invitation I think long and hard about, torn as I am. I have tonsillitis; the outing will demand considerable riding in the terrifying city traffic; George and his friend are avid mountain bikers, even do some racing, whereas I am only a bicycle commuter and have not bestridden a mountain bike in three years. But my strong urge for cardiovascular exercise—outside of coffee the most effective mood-altering agent available within my private system of regulation—wins the day, and outfitted in my dress socks and loafers, borrowed bicycle shorts, and collared short-sleeved shirt I set out on an ill-fitting pink "Penny Lane" model technically belonging to Alice.

There are other signs of something wrong—some visible only to Paula, such as the fact that George and Alice speak not a single word to each other—and some visible only to me, like the cigarettes, the gusto he performs with deep audible breaths at rest points on our bike ride in the forest, the way he drinks beer at the roadside café, fast and smacking his lips, all of which betray a resolution to relish every one of the few remaining sources of enjoyment available to a man of his station, his predicament.

Paula tells me Alice and George are thirty-six like us, but later she says they are respectively thirty-seven and forty. Each night I ask her what she has observed or found out about their troubles. On the last night in Iași she tells me, rather casually, that the younger daughter has mentioned how a "man in the stairwell" broke George's hand. I can't tell if it's compelling because it's true, or because it issues straight from the mind of a child six years old.

You were really good, George says, with unfeigned wonder. And I—he pauses—admire! The way you descended. It is true that once we head down the logging roads I totally smoke them, on the downhill, that is, where the factor of conditioning withdraws into the background. My advantage is having ridden such trails throughout my teens and twenties, through long practice inuring myself to the sense of alarm that travel on them at thirty miles per hour produces, fifty kilometers per hour, a sensation overriding any amount of pride, competitiveness, or desire in my fitter, better equipped, but less experienced companions. Medical doctors both.

•

Friday in Iași we buy tickets for the tram to Exposition Park and I notice a man with Down syndrome standing in line with us. What nice music this is, I guess he says, referring to the Vivaldi piped into the ticket kiosk. By the state, I think, since market pressure apparently forces private businesses to play, exclusively, the summer's several top hits. I believe he's addressing Paula, but he does not speak pointedly enough to attract her notice.

Inwardly I criticize myself for assuming, no doubt because of characteristic facial features, that every person with Down syndrome is especially kind, friendly, and good-natured, though strictly speaking I have no reason to rule out the possibility that these traits, too, are syndromic. It strikes me that the man—with his salt-and-pepper hair, American flag T-shirt, pleated blue shorts, and meticulously hoisted tube socks—should be unaccompanied. In the United States I never see people with Down syndrome by themselves in public. In the United States they seem most frequently to be seen in the company of elderly parents.

We spend two hours at Exposition Park or Exposure Park—I haven't quite caught the name of it, a good name, at any rate, for an urban park—with Sylvie and with Alice's girls, whose affection for the baby continues to win them favor with me. When we finish playing at the playground, we go for ice cream on, it seems to me, the north side of the park. I am surprised there to find Casa Vânatorului and even more surprised to see, as if for the first time, the *vânator* noun clearly declined in the genitive. Then, as we sit in a gazebo with the ice cream, I see the man again. He is standing at one of the park's many pedestrian roundabouts, rubbing his crown with the flat of his hand. The sun is pitiless.

I did not notice this in line at the ticket kiosk, but he holds in his left hand an inexpensive pair of badminton rackets, with shuttlecocks enclosed in the clear vinyl case. He continues to rub his head, turning first one way, then the other, as the children work their ice cream cones. At one point, stooping, he fixes his gaze on a plum; there are hundreds of plums scattered over the beautifully laid paving stones, a pavement whose timeless and durable pattern of intersecting arcs I have often admired.

The man looks at the plum with the affected manner common to any solitary person who has realized, midstride, that they must now, without any observable pretext—how with dignity to acknowledge that you have overlooked something—turn back the way they came. He continues to stand in the broad sun, from time to time rubbing his head. I see him turn, take several steps, kick a plum—though not the one he was looking at earlier—and resume rubbing his head. The gestures have an inorganic quality, as if signaling a consternation he recognizes as appropriate but does not feel.

•

The Romanian urban roadway varies from fresh asphalt to loose cobbles to rocks and dust, with most everything in between, but the better ones are divided and subdivided by a variety of dashed lines or medians, sometimes distinguished from one another by the length or frequency of the dashes. As in the United States, motorists drive on the right side of the road, but in other respects traffic dynamics differ. For example—I don't pretend to understand the rules—a typical highway has four lanes divided by three medians, long dashes in the center, short dashes on either side. Slower automobiles center themselves over the short-dashed lines so that their bulks are evenly distributed in both rightmost lanes.

George is playing some kind of very irritating and, to me, terrifying game against Alice, who drives in front of us. He speeds behind her, tailgating more and more closely until the cars' bumpers touch. George, you're making me uncomfortable, I speak up. He coughs or laughs. Why, he says. He says why as if it were an unfamiliar word. Because if something happened, I say, we could have a very bad accident this way. The children could be injured, I say. Wordlessly and after a slight delay that I experience as an affair of honor, George backs slowly off the Škoda's bumper.

Animals led, ridden, or driven, and horse carts, of which there are many, composites of welded steel and rough-hewn wood—the traces are often simply stripped saplings or trunks of small trees, the horse carts at this time of year carry forage or watermelons, soon they will be heaped four and five meters high with hay—are confined to the rightmost lane. Faster vehicles move in the lane an American would call the left lane, except when passing another vehicle, a maneuver that requires them to straddle the middle two lanes, their own "left lane" and the left lane belonging to oncoming traffic, so that despite the existence of four lanes, vehicles traveling in opposing directions must frequently, if not constantly, occupy the same two lanes, competing for space in a game of chicken that I find upsetting.

"Schedule chicken," the prose says, practice peculiar to the corporate sphere, in which various collaborating teams, none wanting to appear less aggressive, pledge increasingly unattainable delivery dates for their portion of a given project. "Thursday it is," the prose says.

Then on the road from Iași to Rotunda I see a stray dog crossing, every part of whose body communicates pain, shame, and uncomprehending sorrow. To the base of his tail some person or group of people has fastened three two-liter plastic bottles partially filled with pebbles.

I don't like this, George says in English, gesturing toward the animal. And, I don't understand why just to make more evil. This is why I don't like the hunting.

We are digesting a breakfast of pork chops, George and I, but I decide not to air the radical and probably disturbing view that industrialized production of a pork chop is incomparably crueler than shooting a deer through the lungs. Meat production here is less industrialized, maybe not at all industrialized; for the moment George and I might agree that seeing this dog has caused us more particular discomfort than any idea of fate regarding faceless deer or pigs.

I imagine gouging out the eyes of the man who, in a mean drunk, mistreated the dog, but as the dark blood wells around my thumbs I begin to wonder whether the figure pinned beneath my knees is one of the boys from the park.

I think about previous visits to Iași. Once we spend the night at the Rusus', where I am traumatized by the sight of their dog, Cruyff, in his tiny cage. Here is a Rottweiler with an expensive genome, caged on a mountain of his own shit, a close chain-link cage in the corner of a large fenced yard. It so upsets me that apparently at our luncheon of sliced salt beef, salt pork, and sausage, chicken and veal schnitzel, sliced cheese, and pickles, our hosts take note. Afterward, clearly on instruction from Corina, Doru and Corina's son leads me to Cruyff's cage. He opens the door and tosses in a handful of cold cuts and sliced bread, but the Rottweiler doesn't react. You see? he says indignantly, groping for words, he doesn't do anything!

The butchers' dog of Rottweil: first shepherding the animals, then carting their meat to market.

As George's car manages the noisy transition from asphalt to the gravel surface of the village road, I try to ease the emotions—which I am not sure even how to name—provoked by the sight of the dog with the three bottles tied to his tail. Pity and sorrow, if I can use such terms for a body state significant chiefly because I find it intensely uncomfortable, a discomfort I now try, as I say, to alleviate—the only effort I make, as opposed to some effort to change the world. The bottles are visibly abraded and battered, as though attached in this manner they have traveled long distances. I try to visualize the dog finding shelter and with deft front teeth gnawing the poly cord that binds them.

I try to visualize some kind person helping the dog, tempting his approach with a piece of meat, catching hold of him firmly but gently, and cutting the mortifying bottles free. But of course the dog has been tempted in this manner once before.

I visualize the tail blackening and falling painlessly away at the ligature, the dog feeling relief or joy at having been thus freed. But a sound like thousands of plastic bottles scraping the ground intrudes on the rumination and I find myself surveying an infinite abandoned city of the Eastern Bloc, a version of hell in which huge packs of dogs run ceaselessly, dogs of all pedigrees, each trailing a cluster of plastic bottles.

Bringing myself up, I observe that the discomfort of having seen the dog is not so intense now as in the first moments and it is this thought alone that brings me some relief. The image is fading, I think, though I can still see it vividly and painfully, the dog crossing over and over with the three bottles tied to its tail.

The feeling is diminishing, I reassure myself. The pity is going away.

•

The last meal in Rotunda is a hasty lunch Paula and I eat alone in the kitchen, a plate of salted smoked meats with sliced cucumbers, pale green peppers, and tomatoes, as well as a basket of fresh bread, none of which I pay any mind, since Elvira also digs from the garden two dozen small white potatoes and several whole young garlic plants. The potatoes she peels and boils; the garlics she macerates in a large mortar with oil and water, producing a white sauce spliced together by tender pieces of the green vascular tissue of the tops. I eat as much of this sauce as possible, fitting it atop the potatoes, which are cool and of a creamy consistency, without granularity. To drink I have five glasses of mineral water with rose syrup homemade by Gabriela, cold mineral water with syrup made from the petals of a twining rose bred expressly for that purpose, according to what I understand Gabriela to say.

After I eat most of the potatoes and all of the sauce we go for a walk to the river Siret, which runs through the villages of Rotunda, Buruienești, Doljești, and Adjudeni. The steeples of each village church are visible from the low plain, fringed with poplars, through which we walk to reach the footbridge. I take the baby out of the stroller and, not without trepidation, but feeling I should make the effort, set out across the bridge, which is built from planks, wire, and slender sapling piles. It stretches about a hundred meters across the swollen river. A steel cable serves as handrail. Paula and her mom follow me, neither seeming alarmed, something which might put another man at ease, but all I can think about is how, once the sun-bleached planks give way, I cannot possibly be responsible for both the baby and Paula, who does not yet know how to swim.

First, thinking to distribute our weight more generally over the span, I walk faster, but then I stop and make it known that I want to turn back in order to continue our walk along the levee, which we do, Elvira again making the face that seems to denote respectful incomprehension. Just upstream I see a group of boys fishing with long poles.

On the levee the day grows hot, humid, and bright. The wind vanishes from the floodplain. I try to pace myself, meaning not to sweat extraordinarily, watching my feet in their conspicuous sandals shuffle over river pebbles and dust. There appears a bird like a goldfinch but more colorful, I guess it is a European goldfinch, but when I point it out to Paula, it is not there anymore. In a hollow formed by weeds around the large concrete blocks of the old levee, a project Paula's grandfather was involved in forty years ago and which now stands in the shadow of the new levee like a mysterious causeway, I see a lean German shepherd which I feel sure has a litter of puppies there, though I can't say why. Maybe its posture expresses a maternal steadfastness.

Then a figure appears, headscarf, tanned, wrinkled face and neck, a handsome face, shirt with soldierly snaps, straps, and pockets, then neat khaki trousers, cresting the levee and walking toward us on the path, along which we are now returning to the village. She leads a girl of five who is eating a product that to put it in American terms looks like a cross between Funyuns and Hot Fries, one of the infinite worldwide variety of aggressively marketed foods or food surrogates made from vacuum-puffed refined corn and wheat flours, hydrogenated soybean oils, and salt, branded or differentiated by shape, artificial color, and artificial flavor. As we converge, the woman, who has not visibly reacted to my wave, addresses me in a cogent but mumbling stream. I see that she has lost all teeth but one, a lower incisor now resembling a guest standing awkwardly to leave. I smell liquor, which seems to me to account for the teeth, though I can't say precisely how.

Of course gum disease is how people lose their teeth usually, and alcohol has an astringent quality that can, by long usage, damage the soft tissue of the mouth, particularly the gums. Habitual vomiting does a number on your molars. But I wonder if the real factor is how a committed relationship to alcohol affects prioritization of things like brushing and flossing, in terms of time management and of maintaining a personal supply of brushes and floss.

I interrupt her, doing my best to smile, feeling as always that this results in a "pained" smile—the more solicitous I wish to be, the more pained I appear—and say in my best Romanian that I don't speak or understand the language. The woman draws her head back slightly as if to take my measure. At once she says, "you are the mayor's son-in-law," using a word I don't recognize for what I assume is "son-in-law." Yes, I say. She stoops over the stroller and commences to pinch, gently, the baby's cheeks, forearm, legs, feet, and stomach, more and more rapidly moving from one spot to another, as though she has been wanting for a long time to touch a baby, or as though she expects never to touch one again.

Then she takes the hand of the girl of five—who exhibits the resigned self-possession peculiar to children of addicts—the hand that holds the bag of junk food, and, pushing it toward the baby's face so that the girl is yanked also into a stooping posture, begins a protracted effort to withdraw a crisp for the baby. But at that moment Paula catches up with me and says, with a sharpness I have not heard in her voice before, no, don't give her that. It makes me wonder if there is some history between the women, or maybe Paula is different with strangers now she is a mother. I turn to the woman with what I hope is a friendly look—I don't know whether to call it reassuring or apologetic or a look of appeasement—maybe it communicates none of these things. As I watch her eyes I have the shocking but increasingly commonplace realization that she is in fact some years my junior.

That night as I lie in bed, I notice it has been twenty-four hours since I've remembered the dog with the bottles tied to its tail. Not even when we take Sylvie across the street to see the neighbor's cow and pigs and I see the chow mix thrashing at the end of a chain just long enough to reach fully into, or fully out of, the scrap lumber doghouse, onto the bare earth turned continually by these exertions, does the dog with the bottles tied to its tail come to mind. I think of the German shepherd in the chain-link enclosure outside Topeka, standing always on top of its plywood doghouse, presumably since that is at least to do something or to be somewhere.

Which dog suffers less? And how much less is the suffering of the pigs in their dark pen, or the cow in hers? What to these creatures are light and freedom, weighed against security and feed? At least they will be spared the long and terrifying ride in the stock trailer, the only place I ever see American pigs, their loose stool threading the wind, streaming out from the punched aluminum sides, the animals so crowded they cannot lie down, a percentage dying in transit.

I think of the research animals—mice, dogs, pigs, primates—on whom our present comfort depends, creatures who do not so much give up their lives as accept living hells in order that we might have toothpaste or shaving cream or cell-free fetal DNA studies. Maybe what most preoccupies me during this and other of my life's major periods are the moods of animals.

•

On returning to Roman I learn that, in an apparent change of plans, we will attempt to travel to Neptun, a town that, together with Jupiter, Saturn, and perhaps others, clusters on the coast of the Black Sea, near the Bulgarian border.

This excites me especially because we'll be making the ten-hour trip in a sleeper car, and the prospect of being in bed, sleeping, on a train traveling to a new place gives me intense pleasure. It is information about my temperament, I think, that for me the highlight among highlights of a sojourn abroad should be sleeping—an estranged, defamiliarized form of sleeping that makes the act freshly perceptible, and in that sense literary—but sleeping all the same.

Especially intense, therefore, is the disappointment, self-pity, and rage I feel when Paula returns from the train station to tell me not only that they arrived too late—far too late, she says, to secure a sleeper cabin, news that to me clearly and emphatically demands immediate cancellation of the trip—but that they have gone ahead and purchased seats for everyone, me, Paula, her mother, her sister, even Sylvie, on the overnight train. Paula holds the tickets up to show me that the clerk, as a special favor, has canceled seat 91, so that we'll have 92, 93, 94, 96, and 98, a whole compartment to ourselves.

What about 95 and 97, I say, petulantly, despite my effort to accept the new reality and to maintain a pleasant and easygoing demeanor. Paula reacts to this, it seems to me, as though since no one else and especially not the clerk has pointed out in the series 91–98 the presence of 95 and 97, then it is somewhat silly and petty for me to do so. And we do, in fact, boarding the train at 20:00 the next night, find that our party of five has the entire compartment to ourselves. It is not until 22:30, when Sylvie has initiated meltdown, that, smelling strongly of fruit brandy, two pensioners enter our compartment and squeeze into their seats by the window. Not much later, when I want this window open, I find myself in a democratic minority, a coalition of one. "New reality," the prose repeats.

I go out into the main space—the *vagon comun* as opposed to the *salon*—and take an empty seat while the car clouds with tobacco smoke. When I try to access the space between cars, where the restrooms are located, I find the sliding door jammed shut. Trying angrily to budge it, I trigger a muscle spasm in my back. To my relief, there is an open window in the hallway outside the salon, and with an awkward hitch or kink in my posture I stand here watching the stuck door, on which a succession of men vent their anger.

The bathroom on the car's other end is accessible, though I discover there a brimming steel toilet that slops its ghastly chowder onto the floor in apparently random responses to acceleration of our reference frame. Shouting has broken out between the conductor, who appears somehow on my side of the door, and a man just boarded on the other side, unable to reach his seat. It seems to me that the conductor instructs him, painstakingly, in the location of a release button, and the door is finally opened. In the meantime, I determine that even with one functioning door the car would be virtually impossible to escape, for example in case of fire.

The rest of the ride is frankly unpleasant. Paula, whose lap is the only place Sylvie will attempt sleep, has a much rougher go of it than I. When it is over we walk thirty minutes from the train station to the hotel, Hotel 2D, a name that even to Romanian ears must sound like a rejection status, and at about 06:00 we crowd into the one available room. Gabriela and Elvira's will not be ready until after lunch.

It is incredible to me, I mutter, to Paula I guess, that it should be impossible to design beneath a balcony guardrail an open space too small freely to admit a baby, a toddler. And yet most Romanian balconies, in fact most Romanian barriers or guardrails of any sort, suggest this is the case, or else that if it is possible, it is not thought to be advantageous.

Everyone, at this point, is in a poor frame of mind. I entertain bitter and shameful thoughts about how my wife can do nothing correctly, despite the fact that my wife is so intelligent and coolly competent that I have sometimes, in my more suggestible moments, wondered if she was a spy. Then Elvira lets Sylvie out on the balcony and

Paula explodes at her, ordering her and Gabriela out of the room—to go where or do what, in their exhausted condition, I don't know. They leave. We—the nuclear family—fall asleep on the starched 2D linen.

As I "drift toward sleep" I realize I am doing wrong—that the situation demands on my part some display of solicitude toward my ejected mother- and sister-in-law, various versions of which begin to play out in an entertaining hypnagogic cartoon. After three hours I wake with fresh determination to be pleasant and easygoing at all times, at least for the remainder of the trip, a trip whose end I now regard as tangible, which lends me necessary strength.

Just as this end has come into view, and just as the most desperate sensations of self-pity and frustrated rage are subsiding, a curious new feeling comes over me: that this trip, stressful though it has been, was somehow unavoidable, and that my future, if I am lucky, holds many similar trips, each similarly unavoidable. Trying to imagine what I might say to Paula, in order adequately to express why these trips are unacceptable, I find I cannot express it even to myself.

We walk along the obstinately rectangular shore of Lake Neptun, reservoir of lily pads and Tuborg cups, over the footbridge spanning the channel that links it to Lake Jupiter, and out onto the coarse sand of the beach, which turns to loose rock at the shore and then slopes swiftly to chest depth.

By the time we return for a second nap, I feel our spirits have been restored, and no further wrath erupts until the next morning, when I accuse Paula of incompetence in leading us out to the main street for a snack as though she knew somewhere to go, when in fact there are only more of the horrible tourist restaurants like carnivorous plants that grow by the train station and subsist on the steady influx of uninformed travelers. The wholesome, delicious food is down on the beach. My anger at Paula is probably unfair, as is hers, to a lesser extent, with me, and we move forward without further process. I see that I am nearing the end of my notebook. I resolve to be easygoing and pleasant and to do my best to record my impressions of the Black Sea.

Into the metal frame of the hotel's fire evacuation plan someone has tucked a card bearing the image of six martyred saints—a reproduction, it says on the back, from works housed in the Bucium Monastery, Iași—depositing it here, I guess, for someone like me to notice and take into his possession, in the hope he be susceptible to religious feeling and, at length, salvation. But once I have placed the card in the trademark pocket of the expensive and, I feel, pretentious little notebooks I carry, I have second thoughts. Maybe the icon has been entrusted with a security function the fire evacuation plan is thought incapable of performing, though law requires the plan's prominent display.

A resort on the Black Sea, I feel, has infinite literary potential. At times I can almost convince myself I have traveled back into the novel's golden age—as when, for example, I notice how all the guests of the sprawling hotel gather in the lobby, under a pall of tobacco smoke. Of course this is only because no other part of the complex has Wi-Fi. While Sylvie naps under Elvira's supervision, I return to sit there, amazed to feel myself in an atmosphere of mutual acknowledgment, if not congeniality, among fellow travelers.

Also, after I decide it is too risky to take my one pair of glasses to the beach, I feel acutely that the condition of being weak eyed, being without one's spectacles, is a historical one, an anachronism. As we walk the kilometer around Lake Neptun and down to the beach, I marvel at what I can see: in the background, various proportions of green, blue, spots of fluorescent color hanging in the blue, kites, variegations of green on the brown lake surface, lily pads; approaching and receding against this background, figures, brown-skinned or red-skinned or both, whose features, especially their bare torsos, appear as if airbrushed—and therefore, by the prevailing aesthetic logic of my day, enhanced—and maybe because I can't see their faces clearly, can hardly see their eyes at all, I feel an unusual degree of impunity in casting my own gaze, which I imagine as the goggling, depthless gaze of a blind man in olden times, a thin, paunched, gray-bearded and doddering man of forty, olden times. In this myopic condition I spend more time than is strictly necessary, since I find I enjoy it.

•

I conceive the idea of digging a really big hole for Sylvie— the idea that she will love this—so I set about it as I know just how, choosing the right spot, the berm crest at the upper limit of the beach face, excavating with one hand a vertical tunnel the length and diameter of my arm, there reaching the groundwater, which rapidly eases the work by opening the base of the tunnel into a large sloshing cavern. Now it takes all my effort to remove the wet sand apace with the undermining action of the groundwater. I switch arms several times, adjusting my head to keep Sylvie, whom I have been assigned, in view. I see that my wedding ring is brightly scoured by the work.

I find myself at the threshold of being wholly drawn into my task of digging and absorbed, a recognition accompanied by what I can describe only as a pleasant sense of alarm. For a moment I forget about the child and about my status as a family man altogether. I raise my head suddenly, though with great reluctance.

Sprinting past me is the lifeguard I noticed earlier, who seems such a perfect example of the form ca. 1991, maybe because without my glasses his skin is a perfectly uniform expanse of deep reddish brown, his sunglasses totally generic, but at the same time unmistakably the pattern of the Ray-Ban Wayfarer, his coiffure a featureless wedge grading from brown to gold. "White gold," the prose says. He skids, stops, then sprints past me again, his movements those of a young man whose long-awaited test of mettle has arrived unexpectedly.

As if to mock my confidence that the cliché is perfect and complete, now with a liquid overhand movement he yanks off his white-on-red cross T-shirt and, securing a yellow foam float under his right arm as he goes, darts into the waves, where I lose him among the massed silhouette of bathers.

I look back at the beach, which appears changed in a subtle but apprehensible way. Every head has turned to look at the same general spot on the water, a phenomenon I can't articulate to myself without reference to heliotropic flowers, magnetized iron filings, Chladni figures—all, it seems to me as my mind staggers in the grossly slowed time flow of the crisis, clichés at home in the nineteenth century of my hotel lobby fantasy—and now I watch the bathers intently, unable to pick out detail. "They came unto a land," the prose says, "In which it seemed always afternoon."

I see a knot of pale bodies moving in concert, forcefully, toward the sand, and in one arm rising aloft out of the group I perceive the unmistakable spasmodic motion of an animal dying, something that looks to me like noise in the motor nerves. The arm seems to have a gray or livid tone that sets it apart in the blur. Then the knot of men is absorbed into a crowd on the shore, the point on the crowded beach where the people are most closely congregated, and where the Chladni effect is most pronounced.

Urgently but without shouting, not really looking at her, I instruct Paula to stick close, explaining that the crowd dynamic is about to change, that we must prepare for greater confusion. What, she shouts. Someone is having trouble in the water, I say. There is about to be a lot of confusion on the beach. Having trouble, she asks. Yeah, I say, you see how all those people are filming with their phones. I think this might be a good time to go.

I am holding Sylvie very tightly but she does not struggle. Maybe we were ready to go anyway. I ask if we can walk closer to the place where I believe the luckless swimmer is. You too, Paula says, meaning I'm not sure what, gesturing with her head, a sweeping motion that takes in all the staring people around us. "Agony column," the prose says.

We pass the center of the commotion. I see a characteristic image or image fragment: the broad, totally relaxed expanse of a man's belly, round with omental fat, quivering at the hundred compressions per minute taught for CPR. It is the only case I know of a tempo having a mnemonic: the 1977 hit theme to *Saturday Night Fever*. I can't seem to help subvocalizing the song as I gawk at the quivering belly of the man, the dead man, I am sure, since ten minutes at least must have passed already.

On the way back to the hotel—a trip which has the affect of flight—we stop to eat lunch in a beachside restaurant. I watch the silhouettes of house sparrows traverse the red tarp just over our heads. Beneath it the entire dining area is cast in an unsettling glow, like an amateur stage production of hell. I order the *salau*, because Paula says it is a Black Sea fish. I continue to experience the *Saturday Night Fever* theme, even though the restaurant is playing a song whose refrain is "ay ay ay, Puerto Rico." Then a song I know I recognize comes on, and I spend several measures in suspense, wondering how this knowledge will be fulfilled. This is a great song, I say experimentally to Paula, who nods as at a pointless remark. "Lady in Red," she says.

Later, in the hotel lobby, "Stayin' Alive" comes back to me, and I grow irritable beneath the constant, inescapable stream of contemporary hits flowing from speakers in the ceiling throughout the hotel's common areas—though to call it a stream suggests a varied or even "ever-changing" assortment of songs, when in fact it is the same four or five songs. Now that I've learned, despite myself, to distinguish them, they seem to be playing from every television, radio, and system of public address.

•

In the latter portion of our visit I feel it is increasingly difficult to register new sensations, to be struck by the particulars of the national landscape. Bogdan drives us from Roman to Sighișoara—a town I believe to lie on the nation's western border—for the ceremony, our wedding ceremony, although my most recent update seems to confirm that the church has excommunicated Paula, so really I have no idea. Maybe I quit smoking pot for nothing.

I don't believe I ever gave the mouse a name, the one I left to die in the garage, though lately in my thoughts I refer to it as the "depression mouse," as contradistinct to the "compost mouse" living in the bin behind our house in Kansas City, the happiest genetically unmodified mouse in the world, who presides over a network of tunnels in the kitchen midden. Every day, sometimes twice a day, I dump banana peels or mango seeds or stale tortillas. Ferment keeps it warm all winter, not that there is a winter to speak of anymore. When I lift the lid I see the mouse's hindquarters disappearing into the mouth of one burrow or another.

"Stock mouse," the prose says, "bone stock." It would be stupid to think of the new mouse as compensating for the old one, even stupider to think of it as atonement, but to catch sight of her fills me with relief and even joy. "Feeling good is feeling good," the prose says.

Eventually the compost mouse relocates to the kitchen cabinet, where, with a noise like icebergs calving, her gnawing keeps us up at night. Then, foreleg pinned under the hammer of the trap, she wakes us one last time with the sound of thrashing and something like a scream, more of a piping I guess, and then after a moment of eye contact I break a wooden spoon over her head. "Small danger," the prose says. "Small mercy."

We drive what feels like west through the large round-about at the edge of town, over the brown spate of the Moldova, and onto the first of numerous poplar-lined single-lane highways that to me invariably recall photographs of a world war, despite my feeling this is a reaction typical of the wrong kind of traveler, wrong kind of American. On our left there rises a high green bluff or escarpment, intensely green in the overcast weather. I see a tiny figure tending several dozen black goats.

We enter a region of low hills blanketed with wheat, corn, and sunflower. I believe that if I note the scenery to myself unceasingly it will protect my mind from the oncoming cars that, speeding by every few minutes, make incursions into our lane as they pass horse carts or Dacias, the widely mocked national automobile. Of course, the most venerable cars, the only venerable cars on these roads, over which the invisible hand of the market has held sway only since 1989, are Dacias. Say what they will, the vehicle yields in this respect only to the makeless, ageless horse carts.

Bogdan is humming what sounds like the theme for *Airwolf.* Since it is from television he's acquired his fluent English, I ask him about it.

What is *Airwolf*? Bogdan says. It is a late-eighties television series attempting to capitalize on the success of *Knight Rider*. Ah, he says.

Then he says, what is *Knight Rider*. It is a mid-1980s series about a talking car, an artificially intelligent Pontiac Trans Am that helps Michael Knight, played by David Hasselhoff, fight crime, I explain, feeling as though I have never before considered the show in terms of its fundamental premise. Ah! David Hasselhoff, Bogdan says. We have attained common ground. "Fight crime," the prose repeats.

In my country, Bogdan says, hesitantly, we are laughing at David Hasselhoff. I say David Hasselhoff is an object of ridicule also in the United States, though I have never understood why.

Not why people consider him ridiculous, that is, but why from among his peers and colleagues they should single him out. There is a famous video of David Hasselhoff, I say, on the floor of a hotel room, too drunk to stand—too drunk, in fact, even to rise to all fours. He is seen taking from the hands of an offscreen servant some cheeseburgers in a white paper bag. He tries to eat the cheeseburgers. Tremulously recording the video is a child who with pain and desperation in her voice refers to Hasselhoff as "Dad."

I wonder whether people like Hasselhoff are targeted more or less randomly because they have for some arbitrary reason made enemies among Hollywood tastemakers and kingmakers—or have simply been convenient to them as objects on which to demonstrate the cruelty that aristocracy must periodically dispense—and that persons in a series of widening and weakening circles of influence parrot their disdain all the way out to Topeka. "Hollywood's reigning celebrities," the prose says.

The child, Taylor Ann Hasselhoff, mentions a job Hasselhoff stands to lose if he can't stay sober, though it is obviously too late for this. One gets the sense that the job was a career last chance, though the only programs that would hire someone at the stage Hasselhoff occupies in his career are those that have evolved for the apparent purpose of humiliating people like him, or Mike Tyson, or Anna Nicole Smith, peace be upon her. And Hasselhoff just says something like—waving Taylor Ann away—"get away from me."

Bogdan mimics my slurred speech, laughing. "Get away from me. Ha ha ha!" Abruptly he straightens his back. In the loud, suddenly evident white noise he composes another sentence. "Well! We are already laughing at David Hasselhoff in *Baywatch*."

•

I think again about the beginning of the part of my life dedicated to habitual substance use, not to say lost to it, about my entomology professor, Mayfield, good teacher and, I feel sure, good scientist, a kind, slightly awkward man who carries one shoulder high, round face, veil-like beard, white New Balance running shoes, prosody and intonation somewhat like that of a child, how each full stop indicates wonder at everything that is the case. I am a research assistant in his lab.

Out of nowhere come large summer raindrops, smacking the windshield, and I admire the changed appearance of the newly wetted trees, especially three large willows standing inexplicably in a cornfield. Now we are beneath another cloud rupture. I try to watch the landscape but the long horizontal water legging across the glass of my window keeps resetting my depth of field.

My schedule is for me to determine, that is the first problem, and my task is to weigh deceased specimens of *Achroia grisella*, the lesser wax moth, so named I guess because the smaller of two moths parasitic on the honey-bee, hive parasites. Honeybees are not the focus of our research, but in 1999 one hears terms such as "Spring Dwindle," "May Disease," "Fall Dwindle Disease," "Autumn Collapse," "Disappearing Disease," that within a decade will be subsumed under the heading of "Colony Collapse Disorder." Roughly half the industrialized world's bees have disappeared. Children work in the treetops, their sable brushes loaded with pollen.

We come to a stretch of road lined by the common European walnuts that look to me like a cross between walnut and hickory. I see a utility pole with a large steel basket like a crow's nest, and then another utility pole with a stork's nest, an affair of many metric tons' worth of sticks. A stork, white with black wings, peers into the rain.

*A. grisella* is exceptional in that physically asymmetrical males attain greater success, generally speaking, than their fairer-proportioned rivals. The crucial asymmetry is not in their appearance, which the name "lesser wax moth" does adequate justice, but in their song. "Song" here is a technical term, since the song embodies no structure complex enough to be called melody and is not even audible, not for us. It is more of an ultrasonic clicking or chirping.

The moth has no voice or vocal apparatus, managing instead by means of paired organs near the jointure of wing and thorax. Sounding in rapid alternation, these signal his availability—so to speak his loneliness—to local females, who then approach or demur, a decision presumably involving calculations of a fundamentally aesthetic nature. Our research suggests that males whose left and right organs produce differing tones or notes reliably attract more females than do males with well-matched tones.

When I say differing tones or notes I mean distinct right and left waveforms, alternate peaks on the graph of the song scrolling in the dark theater of the lab. The room I think of as the theater, warm and humid in an uncannily consistent way, holds twinkling banks of computer and audio equipment. Like the rest of the laboratory, it is suffused with the odor of beeswax and grain by-products.

The landscape isn't moving fast enough. Every time Bogdan veers into the oncoming lane to overtake I feel the concrete and immediate presence of death. We pass a field of sunflowers over which swifts or swallows decimate clouds of flying insects.

In the main room of the lab I weigh their numbered bodies as part of an effort to correlate the information of the song with another conventionally attractive male trait, mass. I think that my measurement of them is the only time their adult bodies leave the bullet-shaped capsules in which they are stored, fed, and maintained, into which they are placed as pupae, and through whose airholes they breathe their last. The last breaths are constituted not by air but by pure carbon dioxide, in the chamber where each cohort is euthanized. Why is a question I do not put to myself at the time. "Last known recording," the prose says.

Then, correcting myself, I remember that as soon as the males emerge from their cocoons, which look like woolen pills, we take them individually to the theater and record their songs. And we do not, as I initially recalled, use the captive animal but the recording itself, emitted from a tiny loudspeaker, to attract females in a warm arena constructed for that purpose, another wing of the dark theater. I spend nights in the lab listing their masses, sliding open and closed a hood that guards against the influence of drafts upon the exquisitely sensitive action of the analytical balance, shucking the empty capsules into a tray.

The hills grow larger, large enough to appear shrouded in an atmosphere different from the one parting around our own vehicle, and in the mist I see large dark forests—beech, I believe—covering some of them. If this keeps up we will enter the mountains, unseen mountains. I try to remember if the Carpathians stand between us and Sighișoara, or if Romania has any other mountain ranges.

Good teacher that he is, Mayfield has given me a second challenge: to determine precisely how the male organ produces the song. This is something legitimately unknown. I am sitting alone at the superb binocular microscope, resolved—the one time only I am so resolved—to make a detailed sketch of the organ. I make the sketch, am overwhelmed by the tininess of the thing and the impossibility of manipulating it directly. I fold the paper once, then fold it again, then again. Then it seems that by some unlit process of mind I have made the decision never to think more on the problem.

We enter Piatra Neamț, one of the many small yet urban municipalities I have come to associate with this nation, or with Europe generally, enclosed in foothills. A funicular conveys bright orange gondolas through a gash in the beech forest. Citizens walk in the rain. Then, as the city seems to end, although the landscape appears no less settled or developed, we pass under a large welded arch that bears a common valediction translatable as "we wish you good road." The short form, just "good road," is more common. In black weeds under the arch stands an Orthodox priest, white beard and mustache sprouting from beneath his black shako.

In a red felt pouch in my pocket, in my idiosyncratic dress of this era, thick, rumpled clothing that smells always of the nag champa I keep burning in my rooms, at least that is the smell I am aware of, I carry a "Kinder Surprise"—an orange plastic ovoid in which, within hollow chocolate eggs, the candy giant Ferrero conceals intricate plastic toys. Because of their small, hazardous contents Kinder Surprise are prohibited from sale in the United States, but as an exchange student in Cambridge or Barcelona I seek them out and bring them home to use as containers for marijuana.

The felt pouch also holds a straight glass pipe of the sort commonly called a "bat" or "one-hitter," roughly the dimensions of a cigarette. Now in the twilight of their novelty, glass pipes, as opposed to pipes of wood or brass, are a hallmark of the aficionado. If in 1997 someone passes you a glass pipe things are looking up because the marijuana packed in its bowl is going to be excellent, "kind."

I see fir forests. On the shoulder of a blind bend in the road stands a grouping of three dozen votary candles in scarlet jars. In an effort that results in thoughts of particular incisiveness and emotional intensity, I try to force myself not to think about the candles' function. The cornfields and pastures are getting smaller. I see haystacks made by driving a pole, usually a small tree or sapling, stripped except for a few branches sharpened into stakes, into the ground and piling the mown grass around it so that the stakes transfix a pile rising four or five meters into the air, sometimes with a large square of plastic sheeting lashed over the top.

In their virgin state glass pipes are more or less transparently clear, but their interior surfaces quickly develop an opaque coating or patina of oily resin. Because the two media differ in refractive index, the interface of this resin with the glass produces swirls of prismatic color. Some glassblowers—and there are glassblowers laboring over portable oxyacetylene torches in every college town, caucasoid dreadlocks gathered and bound in blown glass rings—allude to other secrets of this delayed coloration, such as impartition of precious metals to the molten glass. But even if I credited these folk theories I would have no clue what mechanisms underlay their claims. "Time release," the prose says.

In Bicaz, Bogdan's hometown, we stop to buy water at SILKY market. Two shivering children, seven and nine years old, stand in the entry, opening the door for shoppers coming and going. The shoppers ignore them. I watch as they repeat the operation about ten times. When a woman on the sidewalk passes them, looking down as she organizes small change from the adjacent pretzel stand, they run to plead hoarsely with her in terms unknown to me. The woman gives them two green one-leu notes, and they take off happily past the pretzel stand and out of sight.

Like others my pipe has a name, assigned in this case by the person who gave it to me, my girlfriend at the time, the first person with whom I would build a relationship entirely and exclusively around the practice of getting high. In a solemn pronouncement as she exhales the second hit, steering with her knees as we speed westward in her sedan, she christens the pipe "Haarviko," a spelling I know because it later appears in her inexplicable letters to me. I never learn about her family or her childhood or aspirations but Haarviko peppers our conversation like the name of a son, anchoring for me a complex structure of sentimental and nostalgic associations, many of them profoundly ambivalent. Midway through the relationship I discover that she maintains a second circle of friends who refer to her by another first name and do not recognize or honor the one I know.

The pipe and the Kinder egg are the center of my thoughts from the moment I leave my mouse-ridden apartment and all through the moist and fragrant campus in the June midnight, up eight flights to the lab and so forth to my seat at the balance. The mice are exotic breeds, calico, for example. They enter my apartment through broad slatted openings in the back wall of my closet, which communicates with the kitchen of my neighbor John.

If there is one thing in life John prizes more than the two constrictors for whom these mice are bred, maybe it is his blue Ford pickup with camper top, a vehicle he describes more than once to me as "exactly like a jet airplane in every way." "First serious relationship," the prose says. "Man-child." Periodically he throws himself down the steep flight of stairs leading into our dark hallway, then drives to the ER in hope of medicines he dares not call by name.

We pass a derelict factory or depot constructed entirely from poured concrete: clusters of silos; a five-story structure with no walls, only bare concrete beams and floors from which five stories of weeds and saplings rise into the light; huge fallen concrete awnings, the bent and rusted rebar like veins in a skeletonized leaf; a tall building with broken windows. Then we pass what seems to be a larger, not-yet-derelict version of the same. I wonder if they are cement factories.

I fold the sketch of the acoustic organ of the moth again and set it aside, perhaps the only image of the structure ever made. I am not a bad draftsman, but with marijuana the whole mind gathers into the point of its instrument, and the drawing or the phrase or whatever figure is at hand becomes a high-walled maze. This—not so much the being overwhelmed but the failure of resolution that accompanies it—I see now as symptomatic of the mild depression, if that's what it is, that consumes my later undergraduate years.

Two winded men are splitting a massive beech trunk into firewood. The bole is almost two meters in diameter. Two neatly arrayed stacks of firewood tower over them. We are now averaging under fifty kilometers per hour. I see or think I see a dead hedgehog.

The lab is as I say on the eighth floor. I ascend through a long stairwell, cinder block painted over in thick latex, a standard institutional gray-green interior surface, a smoothly pebbled texture like Naugahyde or like cobbles seen from a steeple. Over the sealed concrete floor my steps resound with a latency suggestive of the thousands of perpendicular planes of which the staircase or the representation of the staircase is composed. Graphite treads in extruded aluminum coping, one for each of the thousand steps, my steps reverberating, the skin-like odor of state schools—at each landing there stands a heavy door opening on a partial enclosure about the size of a shower stall, beyond whose waist-high rail shine the solitary lights of a great plain of parking lots and storage buildings or dwellings.

The rain has now a soft, alpine quality.

With the possible or historic exception of grasslands, the Midwest's sole oceanic landform is its expansive hemispheric sky, busy with airliners and storm cells, windborne seeds and insects. I learn that insects do not fly so much as they are blown about. Insects are routinely swept tens of thousands of feet aloft and deposited in distant parts unknown and sometimes unwholesome to them. The summer air is dense with beings in directionless unmotivated flight through spacious privacy, separated not only by distances, but also by large gradations of scale.

We pass the complex where they quarry the calcium-rich rock for the cement factories, a series of elevated shafts and enclosures over a railway winding up toward an entire mountaintop peeled away, blasted until it is thin and sharp like a sucked icicle.

On the other side of the landing there is an identical door—I might stretch out my arms to touch both doors at once—and through it the lab building proper, humming and lit by the fluorescent bulbs which offer significant advantages of efficiency over the incandescent technology that precedes them. They cast a sickly olive light that flickers just above the so-called flicker-fusion frequency, so that although I do not see the intervals of darkness, I believe I can feel them through the hastily stitched fabric. I know about the flicker-fusion frequency because the fact of its being much higher, neurologically speaking, among flying insects explains why their flight becomes erratic under fluorescent lighting—which is darkness to them sixty fractions of each second in the Americas, or fifty in Europe—whereas around conventional light sources they fly smooth, continuous circles.

These circles are the result of having evolved flight with continual reference to celestial objects, so that the straightness of the path and the uprightness of the insect's body are both defined in terms of holding the object stationary in the visual field. In other words, flying insects try to keep whatever light source directly overhead, and if the light source is nearby this requires constantly changing direction. It is like the difference between a walker keeping a fountain on her right and keeping an ocean there.

The road winds through huge I want to say dolomite cliffs, with floating pillars of mist and fog that look like photographs of the ancient universe.

I enter my passcode, I want to say 1977, on the lock to a third heavy door and then take my seat at the analytical balance. I reach for an encapsulated moth from the tray at my left, record mass to the milligram or tenth or hundredth milligram—I no longer remember the precision or have any gut sense even of a plausible order of magnitude of such precision—tweeze the body of the moth into an ordinary trash can under the table, and toss the empty capsule, as I have said, into a tray at my right hand, to be cleaned and reused.

Fir, maple, great carpets of moss, profusions of a plant with a single stalk and single nearly circular leaf the size of a parasol—I ask about it, starting a fruitless dispute about two native herbs called *brusture* and *podbal*. The spring growth shows bright green at the firs' extremities.

A diligent worker would be able to iterate this routine about five hundred times in a shift, perhaps entering a pleasant nondiscursive cognitive space, lost in the rhythms of the task and complacent in the satisfaction of doing his work well. I have long intuited the existence of a state like this and I wish fervently to be able to enter it, but it is apart from me, and I have never in the line of duty found it.

What happens instead is that with a sigh I seat myself at the balance, contract my lips and tense my jaw, fixing my eyes on the table surface just in front of me—an empty region where nothing happens—and, for a space whose duration never quite registers to me, give myself up to rumination. It has to be done, I don't want to do it, I am supposed not to have any choice about it, yet I postpone the decision to begin. I must begin, I must begin to begin. Then the little platform of these thoughts gives way, revealing a new and less hopeful prospect in which my whole life is obligation to function and failure to function.

More storks, black wings, white bodies, thirty of them gleaning in the stubble, great towering nests—they build only on human structures—usually three or four birds watching from each nest.

Well there is a colorful period of orientation which I spend in continual ecstasy, simply taking in the incredible fact of there existing anything at all, let alone the immeasurable grandeur and intricacy of what is. This is childhood or at least how childhood appears, observed from the free fall of adulthood. I wonder how has this awful void opened, this orbit whose inscrutably distant center is the undiscovered planet of dread.

And if I die, I find myself thinking, before I weigh another moth or discover my purpose, if I die, will it not be like returning to sleep as I do almost every morning of college—a practice marking the onset of what I call my adult life—returning to sleep after an effort to wake that is no less distressing for its being brief and halfhearted? Some traditions hold that the philtrum is a mark left by the angel who, after a certain number of weeks.

What seem mountain villages—though we are no longer in the mountains and I don't know if we are on a plateau— seem like mountain villages to me because of the steep wooden houses clustered together, as if for warmth. The signage is now bilingual—the extreme foreignness of Hungarian similar only to that of Turkish among the languages I've encountered—and occasionally a totally alien alphabet looking like a cross between Greek and runic, which, to my astonishment, no one in the car can account for. The explanations they offer—I have despite all effort grown cranky in the car—seem ridiculous and infuriating. "The writing doesn't mean anything, it's like the Chinese characters of a tattoo." "It's decorative, they just make it up." Do you have any idea, any idea at all, I want to bellow, what it would take to *invent* an alphabet?

I rise from the balance and go out to the landing and withdraw my little pipe and pack the bowl, if it is not packed already, and smoke and sit watching the clouds shift over the nocturnal green of the trees sparkling with streetlamps and security lights. It is during my time in Mayfield's lab that this begins to happen every night, every afternoon and breakfast and changes nothing in its frequency and only slightly in form when I leave Kansas for the first time. "No party," the prose says.

Small groups of people in wet clothes hold up repurposed plastic containers of wild raspberries, blueberries, or porcini, proffering this forage to motorists. Some carry wet infants. Wet children huddle behind the adults. Later I am told these are one of five tribes of *ţigani* originally distinguished by trade: goldsmiths, horse dealers, makers of cast iron pots, tamers of wild animals, and musicians. I am never sure what to do with information given me about the Romani. When I ask, for example, about the Bulibașa whose house stands on the outskirts of Roman, I am told that his ancestors, like those of all other "wealthy Gypsies," had in medieval times stolen German gold. It takes me a moment to appreciate the implication that this gold remains in their possession.

I recall our last scheduled meeting—though I encounter him later, after he's taken a job at the biological institute in Lyons—on the eighth floor, his kindness and gentleness that are profound without being effusive; maybe no effusive kindness is profound. I say, "I'm having some trouble with depression," grateful to have found any expression at all for the troubles of 1998 and 1999, yet troubled by something like conscience that "depression" does not really name my problem.

Later I feel that authorless pangs of conscience are in themselves symptomatic of depression. I feel I can claim depression because I've been prescribed antidepressants, but although depression is cause for antidepressants, I have no real evidence I've been prescribed antidepressants because I am depressed. In order to objectify my distress, which I am not even confident is real, not real distress, I have to see the doctor. And in order to affirm his viability the doctor has to treat me. So I come to tell Mayfield I am "having some trouble with depression," that I have "sought treatment" but that for reasons I cannot articulate, even to myself, I am unlikely to submit the two-thousand-word report on which passing his class depends. No, I do not know why the report is impossible. It certainly isn't as though I have other demands on my time. I have more time than I know what to do with.

An eighteen-wheeler goes by loaded with beech logs and I admire the way the cab has been decorated with tasseled fabric, a practice that seems universal among Romanian truckers, whose rigs are high, square cab-over-engine models, often bearing a *MAN* emblem on the grille. "MAN" is the only word I can recall having seen on the center-pieces of the tasseled hangings, a large triangular flap that divides the upper portion of the windshield.

During this part of the interview Mayfield shows un-characteristic emotion. Antidepressants—he hesitates—I would be very careful. It shocks me that a man of his call-ing would cast doubt on psychopharmacology, but that is what he seems to be doing. My wife has had some experi-ence with this class of drug, he says. He looks at me briefly and shakes his head, involuntary gesture that means he can't say more or has said too much, or that I must avoid whatever it is for which words are just now failing him. I have never thought of him as a married man.

I wonder for the hundredth or five hundredth time, feel-ing as always that it is not worth bringing up, what could be the significance of the red-circled decals that look like tiny speed-limit signs stuck in twos and threes to the backs of certain commercial vehicles, 60, 70, 120; 50, 70, 90. Psychopharmacology is of course my father's profession.

I go home, get high, and spend seven years walking toward the water in minor cities, returning eventually to Lawrence, where Mayfield's lab used to be. One night in April as I walk Zhutchka along the train tracks through the river bottoms where the scent of range burning is on the air it occurs to me I have a question of the sort I always wanted to produce for him—this is what kind of teacher he is—the kind of question that might evolve into a dissertation or a career. As I walk I try to put the question into words.

I have asked how hard it might be to secure steady income in a country where representatives of one's ethnic group are openly reviled. Irritability mounting, I ask if the Bulibașa and his family keep their gold in a bank. Of course not, Bogdan responds. Does the Bulibașa have a gun, I splutter. "I am sure he does."

When these frogs, their common name is "spring peepers," form their lek at the verge of a body of standing water—I think the term is "ephemeral pond" or "vernal pond"; at some point I must realize, or at least tell myself, that I was never a scientist, only a taxonomist, always have been, though I tell myself this only because I am nothing if not a worker in language, yet I am not now nor have I ever really been a writer, not a real writer—there must be some function relating the number of frogs in the lek, the power of their singing, and the perimeter of the vernal pond or the root of its area.

The song's volume, as measured by any individual frog—I don't have the math or the time really to work it out, all I'm saying is that the area of the vernal pond must correlate to its probable life span, i.e., its ephemerality—and *is it not very likely* that the peepers' song therefore contains not only the primary information about the location and fitness, fitness, that is to say vigor and beauty, of the singing males—I was going to say information "for prospective mates" but of course the information is also valuable to the competitors—*but also secondary information* about the size, that is the suitability, the dependability of the vernal pool? For if it is too small, then it will dry up together with any hope for the tadpoles. And if it is too big, then it is probably a *real pond*, that is, a permanent one, containing predators against which the ephemeral breeders have evolved no defense.

The sun strikes and illuminates the still acre of water pierced by the dark vertical trunks of hundreds of cottonwoods and sycamores so that the wood stands on a brilliant mirror whose hue shifts from gold to red as the horizon blocks refraction of increasingly longer wavelengths.

My irritability is changing into sadness. I tell myself that these years are just a phase I am passing through, that the ever-present regret and remorse at not having pursued a more honorable career is just anxiety about reproduction, an anxiety that will not survive my middle age. By the time I have changed my last diaper I will be a real writer, proud of my "life choices." "Just a phrase," the prose says.

•

We have asked the caterer to begin the wedding dinner at the early hour of 18:00 because of the baby, and at that hour the tables are laid with plates of sliced salted pork fat, cucumbers, olives, cold chicken schnitzel, salami, ham, tomatoes, and two kinds of cheese. There is no sign of the guests.

The long narrow dining table has been assembled from a dozen smaller tables placed end to end, the twelfth of which does not fit in the hall and is instead placed to form at the head of the arrangement a sort of serif, a word that probably comes from an old root meaning to cut, score, or engrave. It is on this serif, unaccompanied, that I am eventually to take my place beside Paula, who sits at the table's proper head.

Doamna Elvira ferries in many two-liter plastic water bottles containing wine and the bilberry brandy of her manufacture which I feel must be of truly excellent quality, unequivocally the most difficult drink I have ever had to refuse. Sometimes after they pour the deep purple wine so that it gurgles expansively into the glasses and wafts a smell like concord grapes I am thirsty for days.

Although I know intellectually how important this dinner is in the symbology of my relationship to Paula and her family, friends, and national culture, I enter the dining room in the bad frame of mind. My irritability has reached a paroxysm beginning at lunch, or maybe beginning in the hours of worry in the car the afternoon before. At lunch what happens is, somewhere between arranging the night's menu on the premises of Hotel Cavalerul, where I understand the dinner to be taking place, I bump my wristwatch, unwittingly switching the readout to twenty-four-hour time, which incidentally is standard in Romania.

Looking forward to the postprandial nap—something I believe I need very badly—after I eat my pizza with bolognese sauce at the pizzeria, I glance into my lap to see that it is already 3:45. I wait for what I hope is a lull in the conversation and say to Paula—with a concern disingenuous only because ostensibly for my daughter's well-being—how are we going to get Sylvie a nap before dinner. Yes, she says, we'll do that right after we do this. When the waitress brings out Bogdan's goulash, a regional specialty he's been talking about for days, I notice I have already finished my pizza.

Cy! he says, indicating the goulash, do you want to try it? He is offering me the first bite. I wave him away as pleasantly as I can manage. Three other tables on the terrace are occupied with people smoking and drinking beer. The largest table hosts four generations, of whom the only nonsmoker is an infant. The great-grandfather regales himself with brandy. From all directions smoke seems to converge on my wife, whose perfectly round belly glows through the pleats of her sundress. I feel a rush of anger aggravated by the fact that I can't be sure whether I am angry because Romanians are clouding her air with teratogens, teratogens known at least to the state of California, or because I would like a beer and cigarette for myself. Here where they are cheaper and more plentiful than water, a beer and cigarette might have rendered my every moment a positive pleasure.

On our walk into the walled city we pass a street violinist who is shouting cheerfully and drunkenly at passersby. Are you American, he shouts at me. Later we round a corner and there he is again, standing in front of a curved wrought iron fence with a tiny park behind it, a park the size of a grave. Hey, American friend, he shouts, don't ever marry a Romanian woman! Paula makes an unintelligible retort.

I speak English! the violinist throws back at her, shouting, though he stands very close to us and in fact has his arm around my wife. He is abnormally short of stature. What do you do, American friend, he asks. I feel I should smile and place my hand firmly on his chest and move him back several abrupt steps. But instead I look down, saying—and feeling as I say so that I am telling a lie—I am a poet.

I am a poet! the man shouts, and at first I think he is mocking me, though he seems essentially good-natured. I am a poet, he shouts again, pulling Paula off balance with the arm he is wrapping ever more firmly around her. There is a pause in which I again feel guilty of an indefinite failure to act.

Do you want to hear a poem I wrote, he shouts. No, I shout.

"Shaving," he proceeds:

> When you shave
> The razor goes
> Up, down, side, side.

As he shouts he moves his hand accordingly, vertically and crosswise.

> Also when you pray:
> Up, down, side, side
> Up, down, side, side. But!

He says this with the air of a tipsy prosecutor, laying a finger aside his temple and bringing his chin down to his sternum to fix us with a serious gaze.

> If you do not have God
> In your mind
> And in your heart . . .
> Is only shaving.

He thumps his breast, then shakes his head sadly. I think about the gesture I have encountered in Turkey, a gesture made to indicate overlong speech by drawing the backs of two fingers down like a barber's razor along the curve of the jaw, since the barber is international champion of such talk. Thinking about this I find I warm somewhat to the violinist.

That is a good poem, I say. I am surprised to feel that in saying so I have rendered a professional opinion.

Good! he shouts indignantly. It is my *best* poem!

I look at my watch again and read 3:50, then level my intensest stare at Paula. This is why we are always late, I fume. It's clear to me that there is now not nearly enough time to walk to the car, drive up the promontory to Pensiune Stejarul, put the baby and ourselves to bed, wake, dress, and drive back down to Hotel Cavalerul by 6:00 p.m., though by the look of it this is Paula's plan. I glare at

Bogdan, one of the most considerate people I know, and take umbrage at the slowness with which he goes about consuming his goulash—a dish he's been looking forward to ever since we got on the road to Sighișoara, though this goulash apparently is not among Sighișoara's better goulashes. I excuse myself, ask the waiter where the baths are, and stand dumbly in the men's restroom feeling the heat of the nearby pizza oven through the tile.

When I figure enough time has passed I return to the table, pay the check, and walk at the back of the group down in the direction of the car. Paula informs me that Bogdan and Gabriela are ducking into another pizzeria to arrange for our rooms for the following night. I groan out loud.

There's no way Sylvie is going to be able to rest before dinner, I tell Paula, trying again, cunningly, to put the crisis in terms that will find sympathy with her. She makes no reply, probably because she is near the end of her patience. Bogdan and Gabriela have done things for us— made arrangements, provided transportation, cooked dinner—with such frequency and with such discretion that I have more or less abandoned the task of thanking them. I believe that to show gratitude over a period of several weeks in a vocabulary of two hundred words would require inhuman strength and endurance. Once we finally get back in Bogdan's car and are most of the way up the winding wooded road to Pensiune Stejarul, I steel myself to look again at my watch, which I now see reads not 3:54, but 13:54.

When we get to the room I try to explain to Paula the difficulties of the afternoon as I have experienced it. But the dinner isn't at Hotel Cavalerul, she says. It's downstairs.

I sleep for two hours and should awaken refreshed—Paula brings me an espresso from the bar—but I remain almost incredibly irritable. I drink the coffee, heave a sigh, rise from my seated position on the bed, and deal my head a stunning blow against the nineties-era wall-mounted television. By 19:30, as the guests take their seats, I am ready for the night—our wedding night, effectively, as I try to bear in mind—to end.

I make my classic mistake, stuffing myself with sliced salt meats and cheeses during the hour or two they are available. "Eating his fill," the prose says. When Doamna Corina and Doamna Maria order coffee and light their cigarettes—Kent "HD" in a beveled hardpack—I believe for one happy moment that the dinner is concluding.

I go upstairs to check on the baby, whom Doamna Elvira is watching over. The baby is doing a sort of tumbling routine on the bed, a preliminary to sleep that, if she is not manually restrained, will last many hours. When I come back downstairs there is in front of my chair a plate bearing a grilled chicken breast, a fried chicken wing, a pork

chop, and one oblong meatball—a *mic*, the national grill-
ing object, made of salt, ground lamb, ground beef, and
ground pork, served with mustard. The rest of the plate is
arrayed with seasoned fried potato wedges. There is also
a bowl of marinated shredded cabbage, cucumber slices,
tomatoes, and one leaf of romaine. I finish everything right
away and then watch the guests eat and drink. When
Corina and Maria again sit back, order coffee, and light
cigarettes, I fear it will be a long night.

I look at the smiling guests, who have driven five hours to
be here, and at Paula's father, who for three years together
with Paula's mother has been planning versions of this
event. I rise and go outside to where Doru and Sergiu are
smoking. The terrace overlooks from a height of five
hundred or eight hundred meters the oldest continually
inhabited citadel in Europe, or so I understand it to have
been repeatedly described to me. I have to hand it to the
proprietors for not cutting down the several large oaks
which impair this view, giving the pension its name.

Doru summons me so that he can perform—I think for
Sergiu's benefit—his routine of proffering the bottle of
spirit, in this case a liter of J&B, and saying "good," "medicine," "Drink! Cy! Drink!"

I have the impression that Sergiu is very intelligent. If
I had to account for this impression I would cite his con-

tinual air of resignation and subtle good-natured irony—
or else maybe his large, bald cranium—but in retrospect
the most compelling indicator is that he conceals his ability to speak fluent English.

I go upstairs to confirm that my daughter is still in the
"break-dancing" stage of her repose, which Doamna Elvira does not know how to arrest, or does not care to. She
watches with gleaming eyes. I return to the dining room,
which has now filled with cigarette smoke, and submit
to waves of intensifying self-pity and—glancing at Paula's
belly—wrath. The thought occurs to me that I might be
able to close my eyes for a bit and sleep here at the table,
but when on a trial basis I do close them, I can't escape
the conviction that people take notice of my behavior and
find it offensive.

I order a coffee and guzzle it as the waiter clears the plates.
They bring out my favorite dessert—my token contribution to that morning's conference about the menu—
papanași, a sort of doughnut served with sour cream and
preserves, in this case quince. I look around me and marvel at the prudence of the guests' drinking. It has been five
hours. Not one person is visibly intoxicated. The plates
are cleared and a second dessert is served: panna cotta, a
confection like frozen nougat—not totally unfamiliar—
formed into a loaf layered horizontally with white and
pink, then sliced and topped with sour cherry sauce.

Then I have a stroke of luck. Paula, sensing that the baby is still awake, instructs me to go upstairs and take Elvira's place. You want me to put her to bed and to stay there with her, I confirm. Yes, she won't sleep with my mom up there. To go to bed, me, I ask? Yes.

I make these instructions understood to Elvira by a combination of sign and monosyllable. Then I undress, climb into bed, and place my hand firmly over Sylvie's chest, holding her in place. She struggles for less than a minute before striking up a gentle snore. I am because of the coffee unable to sleep, but—freed from the literally un-bearable effort of straining, hour after hour, to comprehend an unknown language, an ordeal viciously aggravated by the apparent necessity of maintaining a pleasant, alert demeanor—I lie on my back in a delectable nod.

And I am, after an hour or more, nearing the border of sleep when a knock comes at the door. Paula must have brought things to a relatively speedy close downstairs and is now coming to bed. Wearing only my boxers, I open the door. It is Doamna Elvira. Cy! she says, then with an evacuatory motion sweeps her hand toward the dining room. Bidding her wait in the hall, I close the door and then sit on the bed like a man distracted.

I stand up and bang my head loudly on the television. It takes me more than ten minutes to dress and find my glasses, partly because someone—Elvira, I assume—has earlier cut all power to the room by disengaging the key card from a slot equipped for that purpose—I have no idea why—near the door, beside the light switch, a fact I discover when—after turning every switch in the room—I push in the card to confirm it is there. It is really illustrative of how encumbered I am—how much noise I tune out—the sudden racket of the shower fan and the compressor on the small refrigerator brought specially to our room for Sylvie's milk. I recall the image of Bogdan and the clerk lugging it up the stairs.

I assume that owing to some good reason, Paula has sent Elvira for me, but after I come down the stairs Paula looks up in surprise. The tables have been cleared except for ashtrays, pitchers of wine and *afinată*—the bilberry brandy—and bottles of J&B. I have the horrible impression that people are only now beginning to get truly comfortable. "White fury," the prose says. "Blind rage." Again I look at Cristian and try to confront myself with the time and effort this dinner represents. I look at my unutterably lovely wife and try to visualize our marriage as the great edifice at whose foundation I am a journeyman mason. But my sense of self-pity and frustration—the basic matter being that I wish to have been in bed long ago—is too much for me.

I try to imagine—not that any good could come of it— how I might impress on these guests the kind of exertion I believe this dinner, which seems easeful and full of laughter to them, actually requires of me. I imagine leading them on a twenty-kilometer run through the forested hills of Sighișoara, an activity that to me, but for my knee injury—here another pang of self-pity—represents sheer delight. Is this how they experience the present test of endurance—a dinner with five breaks for coffee and cigarettes, a dinner from which one needs to get up and stretch one's legs a little from time to time, as on a transoceanic flight? I survey the guests. Corina and Sergiu would not survive running even to the door of a burning building. I can't tell whether the emotion I feel at moments like this is a form of concern for others who, though I hardly know them, are structurally close friends of mine—or smug self-satisfaction at my superior fitness and purity, merits for which I unquestioningly take personal responsibility.

Then I perceive a concerted movement, something like preparation for a toast. I stand up halfway, then sit again. Paula stands up and I stand up with her. Corina is handing something to Paula. "A fat envelope," the prose says. Doru touches my elbow. I turn. He hands me a small gray box, then embraces me so that the gift is crushed between his stomach and mine. I feel him talking into my neck, and so place my lips against his neck as well. He releases me. Turning so as to be in full view of the tables, I open the box. It contains a heavy fountain pen.

I am surprised to feel my eyes filling with tears. I face the guests and make an inarticulate gesture, ducking my head slightly as I contract the muscles around my lower lip. "This'll do," the prose says. I am imagining everything I might write with the pen, for example how Paula will sometimes take an apple, press her thumbs against the hard flesh on either side of the stem, and split the fruit into neat halves. Or how on the 28th of October she gives birth to Leo.

Or the part of my life that ends with a conventional passage about light falling a certain way, sense of an ending in change of weather or season, mention of the air as though it meant something, Mayfield's remark that insects are equipped not so much with wings as with sails.